# Bother
# Bewildered

## A play

## by Gail Young

SAMUELFRENCH-LONDON.CO.UK
SAMUELFRENCH.COM

ISBN 978-0-573-11063-4

www.samuelfrench-london.co.uk

www.samuelfrench.com

---

## FOR AMATEUR PRODUCTION ENQUIRIES

### UNITED KINGDOM AND WORLD
### EXCLUDING NORTH AMERICA

plays@SamuelFrench-London.co.uk

020 7255 4302/01

Each title is subject to availability from Samuel French,

depending upon country of performance.

---

For further information on both the development and performances of Bothered and Bewildered please see www.gailyoungplaywright.com

Following a public reading of the play in April 2014 by Guilden Sutton Players, Bothered and Bewildered premiered with Tip Top Productions at the Forum Studio Theatre in Chester in October 2014.

The cast and crew were as follows:

| | |
|---|---|
| Irene | **Julia Bona** |
| Louise | **Alison Pritchard** |
| Beth | **Eileen Reisin** |
| Barbara Cartland | **Tiz Corcoran** |
| Young Irene | **Leah Paris Bell** |
| Shelley | **Leah Paris Bell** |
| Jim | **Ally Goodman** |
| James | **Ally Goodman** |
| NHS consultant | **Catherine Bryant** |
| Community policeman | **Neil Mason** |
| Voice of local doctor | **Mark Shenton** |
| | |
| Director | **Gail Young** |
| | |
| Producer | **Brian Fray** |
| Sound | **Abbie Taylor** |
| Lighting | **Mark Shenton** |
| Props | **Annette Clemence** |
| Wardrobe | **Sally Dillon** |
| Choreography | **Pam Evans** |
| | **Hughes and Nick Leeson** |
| Set Design and artwork | **Pippa Redmayne** |

The action of the play mainly moves to and fro from an NHS consulting room to Irene's living room in Act 1, and then shifts to Louise's living room in Act 2.

Minimalistic settings.

Time – the play is set in 2001.

# A note from the playwright

I have wanted to write a play on the subject of Alzheimer's and memory loss ever since my father-in-law was diagnosed with the disease. He was a great guy and we all missed him and his tall stories long before he eventually passed away.

The push that finally made me put pen to paper on the subject came from an old colleague. I knew that both she and her sister had also had to deal with the stresses and strains and the real challenge of dealing with her mother's illness, and when their situation was partly resolved by their mum being found a place in a suitable care home I approached them to see if they would be willing to be interviewed by me about the 'long goodbye' they were undergoing.

They agreed, and so began a series of long discussions during which they honestly and admirably opened up their hearts, and this comedy/drama is in part based upon those discussions.

I will always be thankful to Lesley and Elizabeth for being so generous to me with their time and their memories, all of which gave me as a playwright such powerful ingredients to add to the mix that has become 'Bothered and Bewildered'.

This play is dedicated to their mother
and my father-in-law.

*Gail Young*
*March 2015*
www.gailyoungplaywright.com

## CHARACTERS

**IRENE** – elderly widow and mother of Beth & Louise

**BETH** – Eldest daughter of Irene

**LOUISE** – Youngest daughter of Irene

**BARBARA CARTLAND**

**NHS CONSULTANT**

**COMMUNITY POLICEMAN**

(NHS consultant and policeman can be played by the same actor)

**JIM**

**JAMES**

(James and Jim must be played by the same actor)

**YOUNG IRENE**

**SHELLEY**

(Beth's daughter and Irene's granddaughter)

(Young Irene and Shelley must be played by the same actor)

## A NOTE FROM THE WRITER

The settings for this play should be minimalistic and suggestive, with different chairs, coffee tables and a few accessories being enough to indicate the various locations.

It is vital that some sequences have a detached dreamlike quality.

# ACT ONE

*Romantic music is heard...* Bewitched, Bothered and Bewildered *by* Ella Fitzgerald.

*Spotlight on* **BARBARA CARTLAND**. *She is a glittering vision in pink.*

**BARBARA.** I have always found women difficult. I don't really understand them. To begin with, few women tell the truth.

*Music swells again as* **BARBARA CARTLAND** *exits.*

*Momentary blackout.*

*Lights come up on an NHS consulting room. The* **CONSULTANT** *is sat talking to two middle aged sisters* **LOUISE** *and* **BETH**. *In a dim light we can also see* **IRENE** *sat in her living room reading a book.*

**CONSULTANT.** So, has she often been... in your words *(looking at his notes)* somewhat 'dippy'?

**LOUISE.** A bit absent minded.

**BETH.** *Very* absent minded!

**CONSULTANT.** When did you first notice things were getting worse?

**LOUISE.** Well... it's hard to know exactly when.

**BETH.** I think it all started when she was in her forties...

**CONSULTANT.** That far back? What happened?

**BETH.** Mum lost a baby.

**LOUISE.** A girl. She lost a little girl. She would have been our baby sister. I remember it was quite traumatic for her and Dad.

**BETH.** For all of us. She never seemed quite the same after that.

**CONSULTANT**. It must have been a surprise for her, the pregnancy, at that time of her life.

**LOUISE**. Yes, for everyone...

**BETH**. *(interrupting)* It was more of a shock for her than a surprise! She didn't want it you know.

**LOUISE**. What Beth means is that Mum was a bit worried because of her age...

**BETH**. Dad was over the moon about it, but she used to say to me that people would think that it was my baby if we went out together! She was always worried about what the neighbours might say about things... and the last thing she wanted folk thinking was that I was an unmarried mother!

**LOUISE**. That'll do Beth!

*Awkward pause.*

**BETH**. And then a few years later Dad had a serious stroke...

**CONSULTANT**. Tell me about that.

**LOUISE**. It was awful for him. He'd been such an active man you see – quite sporty.

**BETH**. Before the stroke he'd had a really busy job, and he was a great gardener as well.

**LOUISE**. Afterwards he was paralysed down his right side...

**BETH**. He had to use a wheelchair to get around. There were other complications as well.

**CONSULTANT**. What were they?

**LOUISE**. Mainly his speech. It was very badly affected. It was heartbreaking to see him in such a state for all those years...

*LOUISE is reduced to tears and fishes for her hanky.*

**LOUISE**. Sorry Doctor.

**CONSULTANT**. No. Don't apologise. Please. It's very understandable that it still upsets you. When did he...?

**BETH**. Die? About ten years ago... I think Mum was glad to see the back of him.

**LOUISE**. Beth!

**BETH**. Well it's the truth!

**CONSULTANT**. What makes you say that?

**BETH**. It was hard for her wasn't it? Looking after an invalid all those years. She wanted a bit of freedom. *(pause)* Now I know how she bloody felt!

**LOUISE**. I don't think you should say those things Beth. Dad was a lovely person and– *(she cannot continue).*

**BETH**. I know he was, I know. But it was hard work for her wasn't it?

**CONSULTANT**. Did your mum have much support with caring for your father?

**BETH**. We did the best we could.

**LOUISE**. We all wanted Dad to stay at home, and he did you know, right to the end.

**BETH**. It was after Dad died that Mum started to become, as I said before, dippier than usual.

**CONSULTANT**. About ten years ago?

**BETH**. That's right.

**CONSULTANT**. What was your mum like at that time with day to day things, remembering appointments, bus times, that sort of thing?

**BETH**. Bus times. Huh! She's never had to worry about anything like that in her life.

**LOUISE**. Dad took care of everything for her, all the finances, the bills.

**BETH**. You see, she'd had rheumatic fever soon after they got married, and he was so worried about her that he made her give up her job.

**LOUISE**. It all stemmed from there really... her being looked after...

**BETH**. She wasn't independent at all. Couldn't drive. Never bothered learning. She treated him like a bloody taxi service before he had his stroke.

LOUISE. Beth!

BETH. *(talking over* LOUISE*)* And when he passed away she did nothing but criticise him about that, remember Louise? *(mimics her mother)* "Your Dad never let me drive. I could have learnt". What a load of...

LOUISE. *(interrupting)* So after Dad had his stroke we sort of ran things for her, made sure she had all her regular bills paid on direct debit...

BETH. Became her personal chauffeurs...

LOUISE. *(ignores* BETH*)* We'd fill in any forms or paperwork that needed sorting out. Any appointments she had we used to organise for her, run her there, all that sort of thing.

BETH. You see Doctor, someone else has always managed those 'sort of things' for her. I had the power of attorney after Dad had his stroke because we all knew Mum wouldn't be able to cope.

CONSULTANT. I see. And she's had various meetings with her GP?

BETH. That's right. She's seen Dr Johnson a few times over the last eighteen months. I think she's had four assessments – is that right Louise?

LOUISE. Yes, four in total. Some at home, and some at the surgery

BETH. I had to fool her into thinking she was going in for a regular check up when I first took her to Dr Johnson. I made her think that all pensioners had been asked to go into their surgeries for an age related check up, otherwise I'd have never got her in there...

*Sudden sharp spotlight on* IRENE *stood all alone and looking very vulnerable. We hear the disembodied gentle voice of her interrogator* DR JOHNSON.

DR JOHNSON. What year is it Irene?

IRENE. *(long think)* 2000? Yes... 2001... or is it 2001? No... 2001?

DR JOHNSON. And the month?

IRENE. Pardon?

DR JOHNSON. What month are we in now Irene? Can you remember what month it is?

IRENE. Month? *(frustrated)* Oh... I can't think! I don't bother about that sort of thing at my age. I'm retired now you know!

DR JOHNSON. Yes, I know. Now, I'm going to say an address that I want you to repeat back to me.

IRENE. What for?

DR JOHNSON. If you could just listen and then repeat it back. I want you to memorise it and then repeat it back to me again when I ask you to later on. Are you ready Irene?

IRENE. I suppose so... it's all a bit silly this is. I'm just here for an age related check up you know!

DR JOHNSON. John Brown, Four Walpole Street, London, England.

*Pause.*

IRENE. Shall I say it now?

DR JOHNSON. Irene, can you repeat the address back to me please: John Brown, Four Walpole Street, London, England.

IRENE. John Brown, Four Walpole Street,... London, England.

DR JOHNSON. Thank you. Now try and remember that for later on... Do you know what time it is Irene?

IRENE. It's... er... You've got a watch on haven't you? You should be telling me! I thought doctors were supposed to be intelligent...

DR JOHNSON. True... I'm going to ask you to count backwards for me from the number twenty down to the number one.

IRENE. Backwards?... Oh for goodness sake!... twenty, nineteen, eighteen... fifteen... no sixteen, fifteen, fourteen, eleven, ten, nine, eight... seven... five, four, three, two, one.

DR JOHNSON. Well done.

IRENE. I've always been good at maths.

DR JOHNSON. How about the months of the year?

IRENE. January, February, March...

DR JOHNSON. *(gently interrupting)* Backwards... What I'd like you to do is to say them backwards for me – starting with the month of December and then working backwards. You know, December, November and so on.

IRENE. Backwards? Again?

DR JOHNSON. Yes please. Take your time Irene, there's no rush.

IRENE. What a carry on this is...

*Pause as* IRENE *says the months of the year quietly to herself in the usual order to jog her memory 'January, February, March, April, May... etc.'*

IRENE. December, November... August/September/October... October! December, November, October, October... October... January/February/March/April/May/June/July... August? August?... No?... is that right? No?... oh... that's enough now!

DR JOHNSON. Don't worry. Nearly finished. If you could just repeat back to me the address you memorised before.

*Pause.*

IRENE. Address? What address? You didn't tell me an address!

*Sudden blackout. We are back in the* CONSULTANT*'s room.*

BETH. That's when we started to realise just how serious things were.

CONSULTANT. How active was your Mum before her memory started to fade? Did she have any hobbies?

BETH. Hobbies?

LOUISE. Reading. She's a great reader.

**BETH.** *Was* a great reader. A bit one track though, always the same sort of rubbish…

**LOUISE.** *(interrupting)* Romantic novels. She loved those. You know, Mills and Boon, Barbara Cartland, that sort of thing…

**BETH.** Which never ceases to amaze me. She's hardly what you'd call the romantic type! I can't remember her ever buying Dad a wedding anniversary card…

**BETH** *becomes aware that* **LOUISE** *is glaring at her.*

*Awkward silence.*

**CONSULTANT.** *(changing the subject)* So, when did your mum move nearer to you?

**BETH.** Three years ago, to a little bungalow. She didn't want to move, but we managed to persuade her.

**LOUISE.** We both live in the same area you see Doctor, so it was easier for…

**BETH.** *(interrupting)* We were bloody exhausted! All that driving up and down to see to her at any time of the day or night…

**LOUISE.** *(ignoring* **BETH***)…* it made it a lot easier for us to pop round at any time if she needed anything, to keep an eye on her.

*Slight pause.*

**CONSULTANT.** And how was it for your mum? How well did she cope with the move and being in a new area?

**LOUISE.** She loves the countryside so that appealed to her. She likes walking. She soon walked round the village and spoke to everyone. They all got to know her.

**BETH.** She didn't make any new friends though did she Louise?

**LOUISE.** No.

**CONSULTANT.** What about her old friends? Did she say in touch with them?

**BETH.** Not really. She's never been one for keeping in touch with people.

**LOUISE.** But she seemed ok… quite happy… at first…

**CONSULTANT.** At first?

**BETH.** I think she started to deteriorate a lot quicker after the move, a lot quicker.

**CONSULTANT.** When you say deteriorate what do you mean?

*We hear the faint echo of the* **CONSULTANT** *saying "When you say deteriorate what do you mean" as the lights fade out on the consultant's room and fade up on* **IRENE**'s *front room in her bungalow and* **BARBARA** *enters the scene.*

**IRENE** *is sat reading a romantic novel. She is dressed in smart conservative clothes. She mouths the words to herself as she reads as she obviously finds it hard going. She is watched by* **BARBARA CARTLAND** *who is dressed in her full pink regalia.*

*Silence for a few seconds as* **IRENE** *finishes the book. She closes it, smiles, and leans back in her chair with her eyes closed.*

**BARBARA.** Well darling?

**IRENE.** Marvellous.

**BARBARA.** One of my best novels I think. The hero is such a charmer.

**IRENE.** I love men like that.

**BARBARA.** Like what darling?

**IRENE.** Tall, dark, strong and handsome. And that scene in the stable…

**BARBARA.** Oh to be touched like that again! To be thrown down upon a hay bale and feel a strong urgent body on top of mine.

**IRENE.** *(giggling)* Oh stop it…

**BARBARA.** Oh come off it darling, you loved every romantic minute of it. We all do! That's why my books sell so well. Men not boys – that's what women long for.

Strong virile men. I love men, just love them. I much prefer their company to women's, don't you darling?

IRENE. All of that seems such a long time ago...

BARBARA. *(talking over* IRENE*)* Personally I'd rather have lunch with a stupid man than a clever woman any day of the week.

IRENE. Such a long time ago...

*Off stage we hear* BETH *entering the bungalow.*

BETH. *(off stage)* It's only me mum.

BARBARA. Ask her if she's remembered the honey. It is so good for you darling. Wonderful restorative healing powers, simply wonderful.

*BETH enters carrying a shopping bag.*

BETH. I've just got that bit of shopping you needed

IRENE. Did you get any honey?

BETH. No.

*IRENE and BARBARA exchange disdainful glances. IRENE glares at BETH.*

BETH. Well there's no need to look at me like that. You didn't ask for any. Anyway, you've already got about five jars in the kitchen cupboard. *(she goes off to the kitchen grumbling to herself)* She's bloody obsessed with honey at the moment.

IRENE. *(shouting after BETH)* I haven't got any honey, honest I haven't. Don't be cross please Granny.

BARBARA. Granny can be *such* a grump can't she!

IRENE. Shhhh. Shhhh!

*BETH re-enters taking off her anorak. She tosses it on top of BARBARA and goes and kneels by IRENE.*

BETH. Look at me mum, look at me. It's me... Beth.

IRENE. Of course! It's Beth.

BETH. That's right. Beth.

IRENE. I know that! You silly girl!

*BETH stands.*

**BETH**. I'm gasping. Do you fancy a cup of tea?

**IRENE**. Yes please.

**BETH**. And I might as well make you some lunch while I'm here. What do you fancy?

**IRENE**. Honey on toast.

**BETH**. Again?

**IRENE**. Yes please.

**BETH**. Honey on toast it is then.

**BARBARA**. I quite fancy a bite to eat myself.

**IRENE**. And some for her.

**BETH**. For?… Oh yes, for *her*. Mustn't forget *her* (whoever she is!) Does she want a cup of tea as well?

**BARBARA**. Only if it is served properly in a china cup darling, I certainly don't want it in one of those ghastly mugs she put it in last time.

**IRENE**. *(sharply to* **BETH***)* And china cups remember, not in a mug. Cups and saucers. Serve it properly!

**BETH**. *(biting her tongue)* Certainly. Tea in china cups on saucers coming up *(muttering to herself as she goes out to the kitchen)* I'll hit her on the head with a flipping cup one day… I know I will…

**BARBARA**. Why does she always throw her coat on top of me like that? It really is most distressing.

**IRENE**. I don't know. Here, I'll move it…*(***IRENE*** *hangs it across the back of her chair)*

**BARBARA**. I have to say she lacks your sense of style Irene. I'll wager you wouldn't be seen dead in a coat like that.

**IRENE**. I'll ask her *(shouts)* Why do you dress like that Beth? Why do you have a coat like that…

**BETH**. *(shouting back from the kitchen)* Why do I what?

**IRENE**. Why do you wear that coat?

> **BETH** *enters with a tray with two cups and saucers and a mug of tea.*

**BETH**. To keep warm – it's a bit nippy out today.

**BETH** *hands* **IRENE** *a cup of tea and turns back to the tea tray to pick up her mug.*

**IRENE**. I wouldn't be seen dead in a coat like that.

**BETH** *freezes.*

**BETH**. Pardon?

**IRENE**. I said I wouldn't be seen dead in a coat like that *(she looks at* **BARBARA** *for approval).*

**BARBARA**. Here! Here!

**BETH** *picks up her mug of tea and takes a sip.*

**BETH**. Thank you for that bit of sartorial advice mother. How's your tea?

**IRENE** *loudly sips the tea and grimaces.*

**IRENE**. Too hot

**BARBARA**. Where's mine?

**IRENE**. Where's hers? Put it on the little table. She's thirsty.

**BETH**. How thoughtless of me.

**BETH** *places the other cup of tea near* **BARBARA**.

**IRENE**. There you go…

**BARBARA**. Thank you.

**BETH** *picks up the romantic novel* **IRENE** *has been reading.*

**BETH**. What have you been reading today?

**IRENE**. Reading?

**BETH**. Oh, your favourite! Barbara Cartland

**BARBARA**. That's me darling. The world's favourite romantic novelist.

**BETH**. Don't you ever fancy a change? She's a bit old hat now isn't she?

**BARBARA**. Old hat? Philistine! What a nerve coming from that frump.

**IRENE**. Read some of it to me will you Beth? Please. I couldn't manage all the words today.

**BARBARA**. Yes, please do. You might learn some sense of style from the heroine.

**BETH**. I'll read it to you after I've made your lunch.

**IRENE**. OK *(noisily slurping her tea)* The tea's still too hot.

**BETH**. Well then blow on it for heaven's sake! Do I have to tell you everything?

*Pause as* **BETH** *regains her temper.* **IRENE** *loudly blows on her tea and sips it again.*

**IRENE**. What's happened to my honey on toast?

**BETH**. Sorry, I've left it in the kitchen. Tell you what – how about some scrambled eggs as well as honey on toast? You like scrambled eggs.

**IRENE**. All right then.

**BETH**. Good. I'll be back in a tic.

**BETH** *exits.* **IRENE** *sips her tea in silence for a few seconds.*

**BARBARA**. Don't let her force the eggs on you darling. They're only good for you in moderation.

**IRENE**. Just honey on toast then?

**BETH**. *(offstage)* Scrambled eggs coming up very soon.

**BARBARA**. Remember. No more than two eggs a week in a healthy diet.

**BETH**. *(offstage)* Nearly ready. I'm doing them just how you like them.

**IRENE**. *(rocking back and forward a bit in her chair)* I shan't have the eggs then… You know, I'm sure she's trying to poison me…

**BARBARA**. No!

**IRENE**. Yes!

**IRENE** *sips the tea .* **BARBARA** *watches on.*

**BETH** *re-enters with the meal on a tray and puts it on* **IRENE**'s *lap.* **BETH** *picks up the bowl of scrambled eggs and a spoon leaving the plate of toast on the tray* *on* **IRENE**'s *lap. She kneels by her mum and tries to encourage her to eat the eggs.*

**BETH**. There you go mum, lovely scrambled eggs done just how you like them.

**IRENE**. I don't want the eggs.

**BETH**. Course you do. Just try a bit.

**IRENE**. Honey and toast. I'll just have the honey and toast.

**BETH**. *(tries to feed it to her)* Oh please try it. You eat like a sparrow lately.

> **IRENE** *turns her head away from* **BETH**.

**BETH**. Oh come on Mum… please…

**IRENE**. *(scared)* No Beth, you can't make me. They're bad for me…

**BETH**. Just try some…

> **IRENE** *suddenly explodes with anger, chucks the tray in the air, and slaps* **BETH** *on the head.*

**IRENE**. *(Shouts)* I don't want the fucking eggs…

> **BETH** *reels from the shock and sinks to her knees holding her head.* **IRENE** *drops the tray on the floor.*

> *Pause.*

**BARBARA**. Language darling, language! Remember you're a lady.

**IRENE**. *(to* **BARBARA***)* Sorry about the rude word.

**BARBARA**. Stick to your guns about your diet Irene. I always say that the right diet directs sexual energy into the parts that matter.

**IRENE**. Do you know, I haven't had any sexual energy in such a long time.

> **BARBARA** *giggles and exits the scene.*

**BETH**. You haven't what?

> **IRENE** *does not reply.* **BETH** *stares hard at her mother.* **BETH** *picks up the tray and starts to clear up the mess.* **IRENE** *helps her in silence and then exits with the laden*

*tray. Over this we hear the faint echo of* **IRENE** *shouting
"I don't want the fucking eggs". Lights fade on* **IRENE**'*s
living room and come up on the* **CONSULTANT**'*s room
as before and* **BETH** *rejoins that scene. The conversation
continues between the* **CONSULTANT** *and the sisters.*

**BETH.** I had a banging headache for weeks after that!

**CONSULTANT.** And the language, did she swear much
before all this started?

**BETH.** No, not really. The odd bloody, that sort of thing.

**LOUISE.** I think she just gets so frustrated.

**BETH.** I have to say that she doesn't swear at me at all since
I've accepted that I'm her Granny.

**CONSULTANT.** Is that a recent development? Her calling
you Granny…

**BETH.** It used to happen very occasionally, she'd get
muddled up. But it's got worse.

**LOUISE.** Yes, Mum calls Beth Granny now and Beth calls
Mum Irene.

**BETH.** It was a bit confusing at first, for me I mean, not
Mum. In her eyes I'm her Granny, so that's how it is.

**CONSULTANT.** And what about you Louise?

**LOUISE.** Oh, I still call her Beth.

**CONSULTANT.** No, I meant your Mum. Does she see you as
someone else?

**LOUISE.** No, no… she still knows I'm Louise.

**CONSULTANT.** Is she ever aggressive towards you Louise?

**LOUISE.** Quite confrontational, but she's never actually
hit me. It's more verbal. She can be really nasty and
spiteful.

**BETH.** You see, since I've become her Granny full time
she'll take orders from me. She'll back down, back
off, if you know what I mean.

**LOUISE.** But it's different with me. She argues with me
all the time, and accuses me of things. It can be very
hurtful. Sometimes I wish I was her Granny too…

*Lights fade on the consultant's room and come up on*
IRENE *'s living room. We hear a doorbell ringing loudly*
*and this sound fades and underscore the conversation*
*between* LOUISE *and* IRENE. *It is the middle of the*
*night and the lights are not on in* IRENE *'s living room.*
IRENE *rushes in in her nightclothes and dressing gown.*
LOUISE *enters with her coat on over her clothes and a*
*torch in her hand.*

LOUISE. Mum, I think you've been dreaming. No one is in
the garden.

IRENE. Someone is there Louise... I know it... ringing the
doorbell all night.

LOUISE. I've been round the garden with the torch, and
the only thing I could see was next doors cat. There's
no one there I tell you.

IRENE. ... and tapping on the windows as well.

LOUISE. Are you sure you're not just hearing things? It is
really windy outside tonight so it might just be that.

IRENE. Go and look again!

LOUISE. No! I've checked twice now and I'm not doing it
again.

IRENE. Can't you hear that doorbell going? Are you deaf?
You stupid girl.

*IRENE rushes out of the room. The doorbell is still*
*ringing.* LOUISE *switches on the light.*

LOUISE. *(shouts after* IRENE*)* What does it sound like mum?
What does the noise sound like?

IRENE. *(shouting off stage)* Bugger off, go on I tell you,
bugger off! Get off my land!

*IRENE rushes back into the room.*

IRENE. Get the police Louise! You'll have to fetch the
police!

LOUISE. Look mum, we've been through this palaver twice
this week now. I've even checked with John next door

to see if he's had any bother and he's assured me he
hasn't seen any kids hanging around.

IRENE. Kids?

LOUISE. Yes, kids.

IRENE. But it's not kids who are bothering me.

LOUISE. Well who is it then? Who do you think it is?

IRENE. It's her.

LOUISE. Who?

IRENE. That bloody woman.

*Suddenly the doorbell stops and we hear a woman
singing the hymn* Abide with Me *by Henry Francis
Lyte on the radio in the kitchen.* IRENE *can hear the
singing but* LOUISE *is oblivious.*

IRENE. There! Can't you hear her?

LOUISE. What woman?

IRENE. She never shuts up! On and on. *(shouts to the kitchen)*
Shut up will you!

LOUISE. What do you...

IRENE. *(interrupting)* Don't tell me you can't hear that!

LOUISE. What? I can't hear anything.

IRENE. Shut that woman up for me will you Louise. If she's
not knocking on the windows she's on the radio...
singing *Abide with me*! That's all she ever sings, the
same song all the time. *(shouts)* Shut up will you!

LOUISE. *(humouring her mother)* Oh, right... right... got it...
I'll go and turn the radio off for you then shall I?

LOUISE *exits.*

IRENE. *(shouts)* For God's sake, tell that frigging woman to
shut up!

LOUISE. *(shouting off stage)* I'm turning it off now mum. I'm
turning it off. I've turned it off.

*The singing stops abruptly.* IRENE *sits down.* LOUISE
*re-enters.*

LOUISE. I've turned it off.

**IRENE.** Good. Silly bitch.

**LOUISE.** Mum!

**IRENE.** That silly bitch thinks she can sing you know. But she's rubbish. Rubbish!

**LOUISE.** *(uncertainly joining in)* Yeah… yeah… she is pretty rubbish isn't she…

**IRENE.** Rubbish!

**LOUISE.** Yeah… er… Mum, have you been cooking again tonight?

**IRENE.** Cooking?

**LOUISE.** It's just that I noticed there are a couple of pans in the sink. They look a bit burnt to me and…

**IRENE.** Burnt? No. I haven't burnt anything.

**LOUISE.** Look, we agreed that you wouldn't cook unless me or Beth were here to help you.

**IRENE.** Beth? Who's Beth?

**LOUISE.** I mean Granny.

**IRENE.** She's a good cook Granny is. Better than you!

**LOUISE.** Yes, she is. And she doesn't burn the pans does she?

**IRENE.** No.

**LOUISE.** She brought your tea round again tonight didn't she?

**IRENE.** Yes.

**LOUISE.** It really would be best if you just let her bring your hot food round for you wouldn't it? Like we all agreed?

**IRENE.** Yes. I suppose it would.

*Pause.* **LOUISE** *looks at her watch.*

**LOUISE.** Look, I've got work tomorrow, and it's really late now, so let's get you back to your bed and I'll lock up on the way out.

**IRENE.** All right.

**LOUISE.** Come on then…

**IRENE**. I'm not taking my teeth out though.

**LOUISE**. Your teeth?

**IRENE**. You keep pinching them.

**LOUISE**. *(gently)* I don't. I don't. Why would I…

**IRENE**. You do. And last time you gave me the wrong pair back. Well you're not doing that again. Who did they belong to?

**LOUISE**. I don't know what you're talking about.

**IRENE**. You think I can't tell the difference, but I can! You need to behave yourself Louise.

*IRENE's demeanour changes.*

**IRENE**. Will you brush my hair before I go to bed? Please? I like that… it helps me get to sleep.

**LOUISE**. Of course I will.

**IRENE**. I think it's in my handbag, the brush… is it there love?

*LOUISE gets the hairbrush out of IRENE's handbag. There is a short peaceful pause as LOUISE gently brushes IRENE's hair. IRENE closes her eyes. LOUISE puts the brush back in IRENE's handbag. IRENE watches her out of the corner of her eye.*

**IRENE**. I know how much is in there you know.

**LOUISE**. Pardon?

**IRENE**. In my purse. Don't think I haven't counted it.

**LOUISE**. Mum!

**IRENE**. I'm saving up and I know how much is there.

**LOUISE**. Saving up for what?

**IRENE**. I've got to save up. It's important.

**LOUISE**. Why do you keep saying that?

**IRENE**. *(quite anxious)* I've got to save up… got to save up… *(she stands and pleads with LOUISE)* Promise me. Promise me you won't take my money.

**LOUISE**. What money? I don't know what you're talking about.

**IRENE.** You do.

**LOUISE.** I don't mum.

**IRENE.** *(louder)* You do!

**LOUISE.** *(to appease* **IRENE***)* Oh all right then, I won't take the money.

**IRENE.** *(grabbing* **LOUISE***)* Promise me! Promise me!

*Long pause as they stare at one another.*

**LOUISE.** *(now tearful and upset)* I promise you that I won't take your money.

*Pause.* **IRENE** *yawns.*

**IRENE.** Gosh. I'm so tired. I think I'll go to bed.

**IRENE** *exits. Lights start to fade on the scene leaving* **LOUISE** *in a spotlight.*

**LOUISE.** I'm tired too mum… very, very tired…

*We hear a faint echo of* **IRENE** *saying "Promise me you won't take my money" as the lights fade up again on the* **CONSULTANT**'s *room with* **LOUISE**, **BETH** *and the consultant as before.*

**BETH.** I wouldn't have put up with all of that.

**LOUISE.** Well you don't have to do you Granny?

**BETH.** Suppose not.

**CONSULTANT.** Does she often hear things that aren't there?

**LOUISE.** She never used to but now it happens quite often.

**BETH.** I think it's just attention seeking sometimes.

**CONSULTANT.** Can I just ask *(looks at his notes)*… you mentioned before that she enjoyed reading. Did she have any other sort of activity or hobby that she was particularly interested in?

**BETH.** Not really…

**LOUISE.** Not a hobby as such, but when she first started to lose her memory I suggested that she started a memory book, you know – tried doing a bit of writing to get some of her memories down on paper.

**CONSULTANT**. How did she respond to your suggestion?

**LOUISE**. Really positively at first. She'd happily scribble away, even when I wasn't there.

**CONSULTANT**. What sort of things did she write about?

**BETH**. Come on Louise. Was there any juicy gossip in it? Spill the beans to the doctor.

> **LOUISE** *giggles softly.*

**LOUISE**. As my sister well knows there was no juicy gossip in it, but Mum does have an interesting style!

**CONSULTANT**. In what way?

**LOUISE**. Very florid and romantic really, it reminded me of the sort of stuff that she liked to read.

**CONSULTANT**. How long did she keep it up for, the memory book?

**LOUISE**. Not long, a couple of months at the most.

**BETH**. She wrote in a pink notebook didn't she Louise?

**LOUISE**. Yes. I've brought it with me in case you wanted to have a look at it *(takes it out of her handbag and hand it to the consultant)*. I'd like it back once you've finished with it if that's alright.

**CONSULTANT**. Of course.

**LOUISE**. Mums got lovely handwriting, very copperplate.

**BETH**. I used to try and copy it when I was a kid.

**CONSULTANT**. I'll look forward to reading it.

**LOUISE**. Thanks Doctor.

**CONSULTANT**. I think that's about as far as we can go today. I'll be in touch as soon as possible about the next steps. Obviously I need to have further conversations with your mother before making my final assessment. I know it's hard but try not to worry too much.

**BETH**. We'll try. Come on then Louise, let's be off.

> **LOUISE** *and* **BETH** *stand as does the consultant. He shakes their hands.*

**LOUISE**. Bye Doctor, and thanks for listening.

**BETH**. Bye.

**CONSULTANT**. Goodbye ladies.

> **LOUISE** *and* **BETH** *exit. Lights fade on the room and the consultant is now stood spotlit as he starts to look at* **IRENE**'s *memory book.*

**CONSULTANT**. Your daughters were right Irene. You do have a very copperplate style.

> *(he reads out loud to himself)*

"It was a beautiful afternoon in June and Irene sat in her small back garden…"

> *The spot fades as the* **CONSULTANT** *exits and we hear the echo of his voice reading this line as the lights fade up on* **IRENE**'s *living room and* **IRENE** *enters with her pink memory notebook and a pen in her hand. She sits and is joined by* **BARBARA CARTLAND** *as the echo of the* **CONSULTANT**'s *voice fades away.* **BARBARA** *stands looking over* **IRENE**'s *shoulder.* **IRENE** *reads aloud from her memory book.*

**IRENE**. "It was a beautiful afternoon in June and Irene sat in her small back garden".

**BARBARA**. You do have lovely handwriting Irene, just lovely.

**IRENE**. Thank you.

**BARBARA**. Read on darling, read on…

**IRENE**. "It was very peaceful and the sun was shining. She could hear the birds singing, and in the distance the sound of children playing in the nearby schoolyard and the soothing faint trickle of water in the stream. She sat thinking how quickly life had gone by and all the things that had happened to her over the years since her childhood."

**BARBARA**. Hmmmmm.

**IRENE**. Hmmmm?

**BARBARA**. Not much of a plot. Where is the action?

**IRENE**. I've only just started.

**BARBARA**. Yes I know. But you have to grab your reader's attention right from the beginning or they simply don't turn the page.

**IRENE**. Well I quite like it and…

**BARBARA**. *(talking over* **IRENE***)* I always say that you can't lose if you give your readers handsome highwaymen, duels, three foot fountains and whacking great horses and dogs all over the place.

**IRENE**. Yes, but this is supposed to be about my memories and nothing like that ever happened to me.

**BARBARA**. Virgins?

**IRENE**. Virgins?

**BARBARA**. Absolutely essential darling.

**IRENE**. Barbara, I really don't think that this is going to work

**BARBARA**. I beg your pardon?

**IRENE**. Look, I know that you're a famous writer…

**BARBARA**. *World* famous darling…

**IRENE**. Sorry, world famous writer, but my story isn't ever going to match up to your novels. Oh, it's useless even trying. *(she throws the pen on the floor)*

*(***BARBARA*** picks up the pen, and takes it to* **IRENE**.*)*

**BARBARA**. Look at your hands darling, just look at them. Look at all those little lifelines etched into the palms of your hands and tell me they can't tell a story, a great story! Everyone has a great story in them darling. You've just got to wring it out of your heart and squeeze it through your fingertips onto the paper.

**IRENE**. Do you really think that I can do it? Write a great story?

**BARBARA**. I know you can! *(she hands* **IRENE** *her pen)* So get hold of your pen and start scribbling…

**IRENE**. Right.

**BARBARA**. *(standing)* Marvellous! Now, just run your opening plotline by me again.

IRENE. *(looking at her notebook)* I was thinking how quickly life had gone by.

BARBARA. Oh yes, that's right. You were listening to those screaming children and there was a lot of gurgling water.

IRENE. *(checking her notes)*... Er... more or less... yes...

BARBARA. Let's go back to the beginning again shall we?

*She is interrupted by the sudden sound of a woman singing* Abide with Me *on the radio.*

IRENE AND BARBARA. *(both shouting)* Shut up will you!

*The music stops abruptly.*

IRENE. Stupid bloody woman!

BARBARA. Oh ignore her Irene! Now – we are going to revisit your memoir.

IRENE. Revisit?

BARBARA. Revisit and embellish. Yes indeed. Revisit and embellish.

IRENE. I'm not sure what you mean by embellish.

BARBARA. Adorn and decorate. Make your memories more beautiful, more attractive to the readers. You need to incorporate more interesting events into the plot...

IRENE. You mean tell lies?

BARBARA. Yes... I mean no... well not exactly! We'll just add a touch more gusto and glamour here and there.

*Pause as they look at each other.*

BARBARA. Are you happy to do that Irene?

IRENE. I'll give it a go.

BARBARA. Good! And of course, you absolutely must include yourself as a beautiful virgin. So, when, where and to whom did you lose your virginity?

IRENE. That's a bit personal isn't it?

BARBARA. Which is why it needs to form a huge part of your story. Readers are unfailingly nosy about a heroine's sex life.

**IRENE**. I'm not sure I want people to read about my sex life...

**BARBARA**. *(talking over* **IRENE***)* As long as my plots keep arriving from outer space I'll go on with my virgins! You should too. They're simply divine!

**IRENE**. Well, I must admit that I've enjoyed reading about your virgins over the years...

**BARBARA**. *(interrupting)* And as a historical romance is the only kind of book where chastity really counts, you really have to make your novel as period a piece as possible... throw in some uniforms, that sort of thing.

**IRENE**. Yes... uniforms...

**BARBARA**. Now think back to your virginity again. When did you lose it and to whom?

*Pause.*

**BARBARA**. I assume it was on your wedding night?

*Long pause.*

**BARBARA**. Oh for goodness sake! Come along Irene!

**IRENE**. I'm thinking, I'm thinking...

**BARBARA**. Well! The earth can't have moved much for you that night darling...

**IRENE**. Shhhhhh. Quiet. Can you hear that?

*Very faint sound of 1940s dance music swells and then recedes.*

**BARBARA**. Hear what? Oh yes *(she sways to the music)*. My kind of music.

**IRENE**. It always reminds me of the war.

**BARBARA**. World War Two. Of course! How old were you when World War Two started?

**IRENE**. I was a teenager.

**BARBARA**. A teenager in the war years? How exciting! Oh forget about all those children playing in the schoolyard Irene! We'll aim straight for a war hero returning home in uniform with plenty of pent up testosterone, and...

**IRENE.** No.

**BARBARA.** No?

**IRENE.** It wasn't like that.

**BARBARA.** Aha! So you *were* deflowered on your wedding night!

**IRENE.** *(shouts)* LISTEN! *(pause)* No… Just listen will you. Listen.

*The dance music swells again. Lights dim on* **IRENE** *and* **BARBARA** *and come up on* **YOUNG IRENE** *entering the dance floor with her boyfriend* **JIM**. *They are good dancers and dance the Lindy Hop. The initial energetic music ends, and then the 1940s version of* Bewitched, Bothered and Bewildered *plays and fades to underscore this scene. They smooch romantically.* **IRENE** *is still seated looking on with* **BARBARA**.

**BARBARA.** You were a handsome couple Irene.

**IRENE.** We were? Yes, I suppose we were. I was so happy… and then he told me.

*The young couple stop dancing in the spotlight.*

**JIM.** Next week. I'm going next week…

**YOUNG IRENE.** When next week?

**JIM.** In a couple of days. I might have to travel down on Sunday night…

**YOUNG IRENE.** Jim… no… it's too soon…

**JIM.** I've known for a while. I just didn't want to tell you till nearer the time…

*They hug each other.* **IRENE** *is very upset.*

**JIM.** Don't cry, please don't cry Irene.

**YOUNG IRENE.** It's not fair. I don't want you to go Jim… I'm scared for you.

**JIM.** But I must… I've got to go… That's how things are sweetheart.

**JIM** *wipes her tears away and kisses her gently.*

**BARBARA.** Call that a kiss Irene!

IRENE. I don't know what you mean...

BARBARA. Oh come on darling! Jim's a good looking lad and you were such a pretty girl. Let's see a bit of passion.

*The gentle kiss turns into a passionate embrace.*

BARBARA. Now that's more like it...

IRENE. *(interrupting)* That's enough!

YOUNG IRENE *breaks away, and she and* JIM *are frozen in the moment.*

BARBARA. And then?

IRENE. Then he walked me home.

BARBARA. 'He walked me home'? 'He walked me home'? You'll have to give your readers a lot more than that Irene!

BARBARA *rushes over the young couple who are frozen in the moment.*

BARBARA. Just look at how your young bosom was heaving, at the longing you had for each other. All that young love, that yearning. Can't you remember that?

IRENE. As though it was yesterday.

BARBARA *rushes back to* IRENE.

BARBARA. Then embellish Irene. Embellish!

*The sound of the band music swells as the moment unfreezes in the spotlight.*

YOUNG IRENE. Let's go Jim.

JIM. But the dance doesn't finish for another hour yet...

YOUNG IRENE. I know. I know but...

*Pause.*

YOUNG IRENE. I love you so much Jim, you know that don't you?

JIM. I've always known it Irene. I love you too.

YOUNG IRENE. I don't want you to go.

JIM. I know you don't.

**YOUNG IRENE**. You're everything to me, everything…

**JIM**. And you are to me…

**YOUNG IRENE**. Oh, let's forget the dance… come on… let's go…

> **YOUNG IRENE** *takes* **JIM***'s hands and gently pulls him towards her as the music swells again and they run offstage. Lights fade up on* **IRENE***'s living room as before.*

**IRENE**. I just wanted him so much and…

**BARBARA**. And?

**IRENE**. *(slamming shut her memory book)* I'm not giving you any more details Barbara. That's your lot!

**BARBARA**. You don't have to darling. Your readers will still love it. Always leave them wanting more. A young virgin, romantic love, high drama. Write it all down – quickly. And of course, when he comes back…

**IRENE**. Comes back?

**BARBARA**. From the war. When he comes back you can include a passionate reunion scene with Jim in uniform. Period detail, remember? Very important.

**IRENE**. No. No. Jim didn't come back…*(pause)* He was lost…

> *Pause.*

**BARBARA**. Lost?

**IRENE**. At sea… the Atlantic Ocean…

> *Long pause.*

**BARBARA**. I am so sorry darling, so sorry. That must have been very hard for you.

**IRENE**. I kept a part of him though, for a little while…

> *Spotlight fades up on* **YOUNG IRENE** *holding a baby swaddled in a shawl.*

**IRENE**. A boy. Eight pounds three ounces. Loads of hair. Beautiful he was. I can still see him now…

YOUNG IRENE. Look at you, just look at you! I'm your mum little man, I'm your mum. And I'll be a good one! I promise I will... I know I will...

BARBARA. What was his name?

YOUNG IRENE. James. It suits you doesn't it? James. After your Dad... *(she kisses the baby)*. He would have been so, so proud of you...

IRENE. He was adopted of course...

> IRENE*'s words "He was adopted of course" echo across the stage, and* YOUNG IRENE *lets the shawl drop slowly to reveal that it is empty. She buries her face in the shawl and exits slowly as the spot on her fades. The echo fades out as* IRENE *speaks...*

IRENE. I wanted to keep him but my mum and dad wouldn't hear of it. They nearly had a heart attack when they found out I was pregnant... packed me off to stay with a relative who lived at the other end of the country until it was all over... and then...

BARBARA. And then what?

IRENE. I was back in the fold.

BARBARA. A virgin again?

IRENE. That's right. A virgin again. But they were petrified that the neighbours would find out. It was like this terrible secret... I never felt clean again...

BARBARA. But I can understand your mother and father wanting to keep it a secret darling. Every man in those days had been brought up with the idea that decent women didn't pop in and out of bed. Men would have been told by their mothers that 'nice girls don't'. They all find out, of course, when they get older, that this isn't necessarily the case...

IRENE. I was a nice girl once. I was!

BARBARA. And you still are darling. We all like to think that we are.

IRENE. I wanted to keep James, but they wouldn't let me... they just wouldn't let me.

BARBARA. You should get it all down on paper darling, get it all out of your system and write it down on paper.

IRENE. But it's a secret... someone might find out my secret...

BARBARA. *(gently)* You mustn't worry so much Irene. The world is full of problems and secrets, full of them. But what really matters, and what readers love to find out, is how people resolve them.

BARBARA *exits as* IRENE *wipes away her tears.* Bewitched, Bothered and Bewildered *is heard. The lights gently fade to a half light and a soft mist swirls around the stage. All the movements in this sequence have a dream like quality to them. The music continues to play as* LOUISE *enters carrying* IRENE*'s nightdress and hairbrush. She gently changes* IRENE *into the nightdress, sits her down and then brushes her hair.* LOUISE *tenderly wraps her mum up in a blanket, kisses her forehead and then withdraws.* IRENE *appears to be asleep. The music becomes discordant and is drowned out by a woman loudly singing* Abide with me *on the radio.* IRENE*'s eyes snap open. She throws off the blanket and rushes to the door.*

IRENE. *(Shouting off stage)* Shut up will you. Bloody shut up!

*The singing stops suddenly.*

*Silence.*

IRENE *slowly walks back to her chair. She sits down.* Abide with me *suddenly starts up again.*

IRENE. *(very loudly)* SHUT UP!

Abide with me *stops abruptly.*

IRENE. RUBBISH! That was absolutely rubbish! YOU CAN'T SING YOU KNOW!

IRENE *sits down again, pulls the blanket round her, settles back in the chair and closes her eyes. The sound of someone tapping on the windows is heard very softly but insistently. It slowly grows louder and louder until it is unbearable for* **IRENE**. *She holds her hands over her ears and rocks back and forth in the chair.*

**IRENE**. *(nearly in tears)* Go away. Just go away will you! *(shouts)* I'll fetch the police. I will!

*The loud tapping becomes intermingled with the sound of a baby crying in the distance.* **IRENE** *stands slowly and listens intently. The crying becomes louder. She looks around the room becoming more and more distressed.*

**IRENE**. Oh don't cry – don't cry. Are you hungry... you sound so hungry... you must need feeding. I'll find you little one... I'll find you...

*The crying grows unbearably loud.* **IRENE** *runs off stage.*

*Sudden silence and blackout.*

*Lights come up on* **LOUISE** *stood on the street outside* **IRENE**'s *bungalow. It is the middle of the night. She has her coat on over her pyjamas, is wearing wellies and carrying a torch.* **BETH** *enters similarly dressed and has a torch in her hand.*

**BETH**. This is a bloody nightmare!

**LOUISE**. Oh try and stay calm will you Beth, she can't have gone that far.

**BETH**. Are you sure that you locked the front door when you tucked her in tonight?

**LOUISE**. Yes, and I waited till she'd settled before I left.

**BETH**. We're going to have to start double checking all the locks from now on.

**LOUISE**. I just didn't think she'd force open her bedroom window!

**BETH**. How did you find out?

**LOUISE**. John next door saw her trotting down the road in her nightie.

**BETH**. Why didn't he stop her?

LOUISE. He tried, but he said she was off like a flash – and he's not that steady on his feet – that's when he got on the phone to me.

BETH. Thank God it isn't raining! If she's only got her nightie on...

LOUISE. *(interrupting)* And I don't think she's got anything on her feet! She could freeze to death.

BETH. Every cloud has a silver lining!

LOUISE. Beth!

BETH. *(checking her watch)* How long does it take for the flaming police to respond? She'll have left the bloody country by the time they get here.

LOUISE. It's the community bobby isn't it? He's usually pretty good.

BETH. He must be sick of the sight of our family. How many call outs is it now?

LOUISE. Just a couple. Stop exaggerating will you! Is your Geoff still driving round?

BETH. He's gone to look for her on the other side of the estate, and I can't guarantee that he won't strangle her if he gets hold of her.

LOUISE. There's no need for that. She doesn't realize how much upset she's causing.

BETH. Yes, but she's our Mum isn't she? Not Geoff's! I tell you, there's been some right rows in our house lately over all of this. It's all right for you.

LOUISE. All right for me? What's that supposed to mean?

BETH. You haven't got a husband to consider.

LOUISE. Well excuse me for being a single woman!

BETH. I haven't only got mum to contend with. Geoff and I haven't sat down and had our tea together for months and...

LOUISE. Look, we agreed that you would take her tea round most nights if I called every morning on my way to work to help her get up and dressed...

BETH. *(interrupting)* Yes but...

**LOUISE.** *(talking over* **BETH***)* It's what we agreed! I get her up on my way to work, and you sort out her tea...

**BETH.** You can hardly compare giving her a bit of cereal to cooking for her day in and day out!

**LOUISE.** Well what do you suggest then? Shall we just chuck her in a kennel in the garden and keep her on a lead?

**BETH.** Oh very funny. Very funny!

*Awkward pause.*

**LOUISE.** It's not working is it?

**BETH.** What?

**LOUISE.** Her staying in the bungalow.

**BETH.** Look Louise, the doctor said we should try and keep her in her own environment as long as possible, try and keep her in familiar surroundings.

**LOUISE.** I know. I know.

*Pause.*

**LOUISE.** What are we going to do Beth?

**BETH.** Christ knows.

*Pause.*

**LOUISE.** I don't want her to go in a home.

**BETH.** Neither do I.

**LOUISE.** She looked after our Dad all those years...

**BETH.** And hated every minute of it!

**LOUISE.** ... she looked after Dad all those years. She deserves more than just being put in a home.

**BETH.** So what do you suggest then?

**LOUISE.** I'll have a word at work...

**BETH.** Somehow I can't see them taking mum on...

**LOUISE.** Pack it in will you! This is serious. I'll have a word at work about me going part time. I can take some unpaid leave. Mum will just have to come and live with me and then I can keep proper tabs on her at night.

**BETH.** Don't go making any rash decisions – you should sleep on it.

**LOUISE.** Chance would be a fine thing!

**BETH.** Are you sure about this, about her coming to stay with you?

**LOUISE.** Beth, I'm sure. I can't go on like this anymore. I can't...and I'm not putting her in a home...

*Pause.*

**BETH.** I'm sorry.

**LOUISE.** For what?

**BETH.** For being such a pig to you before. It's just that Geoff's been on my case and...

**LOUISE.** Carry on! Why change the habit of a lifetime?... Oh, come here Miss Piggy and give me a cuddle.

*They hug each other.*

**BETH.** I'm bloody freezing.

**LOUISE.** So am I.

*BETH's mobile phone rings.*

**BETH.** Geoff ? What's happening?... What's that?... You think she's on her way back to the bungalow?...

**LOUISE.** Is she all right?

**BETH.** Is she all right?... is she... *(she nods to* **LOUISE***)* WHAT? Well why didn't you keep hold of her...*(she looks at the phone in disbelief)* Great, he's hung up! He's bloody well gone and hung up on me!

**LOUISE.** What's happened?

**BETH.** He was trying to persuade her to get in his car – near the crossroads – and...

**LOUISE.** And what?

**BETH.** She put up a bit of a fight and ran off before he could get her into the car!

**LOUISE.** Hey... hold on... look... look! That's her at the end of the road.

**BETH.** Mum! Mum!

*BETH shouts as she runs off stage to apprehend* **IRENE***.*

**BETH**. Irene. Come here! It's Granny. Do as you're told now... Come here...

**LOUISE**. Oh My God ! Grab her Beth. Quick. Grab her!

**BETH** *re-enters with a firm grip on* **IRENE** *who is struggling to break free.* **IRENE** *is barefoot and wearing a nightdress.*

**BETH**. Now stop that. Stop it Irene. You're not going anywhere. It's way past your bedtime.

**IRENE** *tries to bite* **BETH**.

**LOUISE**. Stop that.

**BETH**. That is very naughty Irene.

**IRENE**. Sorry Granny.

**LOUISE**. Where've you been? We've been worried sick about you Mum.

**BETH**. Come on. Let's get you back into the bungalow in the warm.

**IRENE** *struggles. She is very distressed.*

**IRENE**. No. No. I've got to find my baby.

**BETH**. Who?

**IRENE**. My baby. I've got to find my baby.

**LOUISE**. What baby? We're your babies.

**IRENE**. No you're not... *(shouts loudly)* Help, they're trying to kidnap me. Help!

**BETH***'s phone goes off again. She struggles to hold her mum and answer the phone at the same time.* **LOUISE** *also gets hold of* **IRENE**.

**BETH**. *(really annoyed)* Yes... yes... we've got her. She's fine (**IRENE** *bites* **BETH***'s hand*) OW! For God's sake Mum! *(back on the phone)* Yes, I know you've got work in the morning!... Well go back to bloody bed then! *(she hangs up in a temper)*.

**IRENE**. *(shouting)* Help. Help!

**BETH**. *(shouting over her mum)* Oh for God's sake stop all that bloody shouting will you!.

*Suddenly a police siren is heard and there are flashing lights and the headlights of a car. The car pulls up. We hear a car door open and shut. The community policeman approaches the scene.*

POLICEMAN. Hello ladies. Problems with your mum again?

IRENE. Who are you?

POLICEMAN. Hello Irene. Don't you remember me? I hear you're causing a bit of bother tonight.

**BETH** *and* **LOUISE** *are still struggling to control* **IRENE**.

BETH. You took your time didn't you?

POLICEMAN. Sorry about the delay, it's been a busy night.

LOUISE. Thanks for coming out anyway.

IRENE. Leave me alone. Leave me alone! *(*IRENE *escapes from her daughters and rushes up to the* **POLICEMAN***)* Help me, help! I'm being kidnapped!

BETH. Don't be ridiculous! Who'd pay a ransom for you!

POLICEMAN. Your daughters are just trying to help you. Trust me, I'm a policeman.

IRENE. No you're not.

POLICEMAN. Course I am! I'm not wearing this uniform for the good of my health now am I?

IRENE. Anyone can get an outfit like that. Where's your credentials!

POLICEMAN. Come on Irene, you can't stay out on the street all night. It's really dark and cold and you're going to…

IRENE. Prove it. Put me in a cell if you're a real policeman.

POLICEMAN. Look, if you don't go back into your bungalow with your daughters I'm going to have to…

IRENE. *(holds out her hands)* Cuff me, go on. Arrest me.

POLICEMAN. Arrest you?

IRENE. If you want me to go back in there you'll have to arrest me and carry me in.

*Pause. Standoff between* **IRENE** *and the* **POLICEMAN***. The* **POLICEMAN** *winks at the sisters.*

**POLICEMAN**. All righty then. *(He places his hand on* **IRENE***'s shoulder. She solemnly listens to him.)*

**POLICEMAN**. I arrest you in the name of the law.

**IRENE**. On what charge?

*Pause as* **IRENE, BETH** *and* **LOUISE** *stare at the* **POLICEMAN** *while he mulls it over. He looks down.*

**POLICEMAN**. On the charge that you have nothing on your feet and could cause yourself untold harm on a night as cold as this.

*Pause while* **IRENE** *stares at her feet. She looks up at the* **POLICEMAN**.

**IRENE**. I accept the charge.

**POLICEMAN**. You do? Excellent! Come on then young lady, let's be having you.

**IRENE**. You'll have to carry me in though!

*The* **POLICEMAN** *picks up* **IRENE**.

**BETH**. Well done. I think that's the first thing she's accepted in the last six months.

**POLICEMAN**. Winning ways. That's what they teach you on the force. Winning ways.

*He starts to carry* **IRENE** *offstage.*

**IRENE**. You're a big strong lad aren't you?

**POLICEMAN**. All part of the service…

*The* **POLICEMAN** *carries* **IRENE** *offstage.* **BETH** *goes to accompany him.* **LOUISE** *suddenly bursts into tears.* **BETH** *turns back and hugs her.*

**BETH**. Hey, hey. Come on now. She's all right. She's all right.

**LOUISE**. But what if she'd reached the main road? Anything could have happened, anything!

**BETH**. But it didn't did it? She's ok… *(shouting after the* **POLICEMAN***)* Hold on will you, the front doors still locked… hang on… I've got the key…

BETH *runs offstage.* LOUISE *wipes away a tear. She looks up at the sky.*

LOUISE. Can you hear me Dad? Can you? I hope I don't lose my marbles when I get old... I'd rather leave the party early than overstay my welcome...*(suddenly clasps her hands together in prayer and closes her eyes)* Dear God, when my time comes please, please, please let me die in my sleep in my own bed of a heart attack with all my faculties intact. Amen *(she opens her eyes momentarily & then shuts them hastily to restart her prayer).* But not for a good few years yet...

BETH *shouts offstage.*

BETH. Louise? What are you doing out there?

LOUISE. *(shouts)* Just talking to myself.

BETH. *(offstage)* Not you as well! Come on in out of the cold...

LOUISE. *(giggles through her tears and then shouts)* Coming! I'm coming...

LOUISE *looks up at the sky and blows her Dad a kiss.*

LOUISE. Night Dad. Sleep tight...

*She stands in the lamplight, which fades slowly. As the lights fade we hear* Bewitched, Bothered and Bewildered *play).*

## End of Act One

# ACT TWO

## Scene One

Bewitched, Bothered and Bewildered *plays.*
*Spotlight fades up on* **BARBARA CARTLAND**. *She is still*
*a shimmering vision in pink.*

**BARBARA.** If the eyes are the mirror of the soul then one's
beauty sleep is absolutely essential…

*Spot and romantic music fades as* **BARBARA** *exits and*
*the lights come up on* **LOUISE**'s *living room.* **LOUISE**
*enters in her nightclothes and dressing gown. She has a*
*mug of tea in her hand. She looks at herself in the hand*
*mirror that is already on the coffee table along with a box*
*of curlers and a comb. There is also a duster and a can*
*of furniture polish on the coffee table.*

**LOUISE.** If the bags under my eyes get any bigger I'll be
charged for carrying excess luggage.

*IRENE enters carrying a teddy bear. She is wearing her*
*hat, a coat, underwear, a blouse and cardigan, and her*
*socks, but no trousers or skirt.* **LOUISE** *regards her.*

**LOUISE.** Is this the latest spring fashion I see before me?

**IRENE.** Where's that little girl?

**LOUISE.** What little girl?

**IRENE.** I like her. I haven't seen her for months… what was
her name now? What day is it today?

**LOUISE.** Friday. I see you've found teddy.

**IRENE.** Teddy?

*LOUISE points to teddy.*

**IRENE.** Baby.

**LOUISE.** Sorry, baby.

*IRENE sits down and puts teddy on her lap to look at him.*

*She listens for a response.*

*IRENE gives teddy a kiss.*

**LOUISE.** I did lay all your clothes out for you on the bed. Didn't you see them?

*Pause – no reply from IRENE.*

**LOUISE.** Oh, just stay there while I run upstairs and get your trousers.

*LOUISE exits.*

**IRENE.** *(Irene sings the song to teddy with all the relevant actions.)*
"INCY WINCY SPIDER CLIMBED UP THE SPOUT.
DOWN CAME THE RAIN AND WASHED THE SPIDER
    OUT.
OUT CAME THE SUN AND DRIED UP ALL THE RAIN.
AND INCY WINCY SPIDER RAN UP THE SPOUT AGAIN".
HURRAY!!!!

*She laughs.* **LOUISE** *re-enters carrying* **IRENE***'s trousers.*

**LOUISE.** Let's get you into these before you scare the horses. Those legs of yours aren't what they used to be.

**IRENE.** I've got good legs.

**LOUISE.** Put baby down a minute.

**IRENE.** They're better than yours.

**LOUISE.** Cheeky! That's right, stand up.

*LOUISE kneels in front of IRENE to help put the trousers on.*

**IRENE.** I'm not wearing those. You've done something to them.

**LOUISE.** What do you mean?

IRENE. You've washed them in that liquid. It does something to my skin.

LOUISE. No it doesn't.

IRENE. It does. It poisons it, makes me come out in big blisters...

LOUISE. I can assure you that I haven't...

IRENE. *(interrupting)* Prove it then. You put them on! Go on!

LOUISE. *(big sigh)* All right then, but I don't even think they'll fit me...

LOUISE *struggles into the item of clothing as best she can.*

LOUISE. *(muttering to herself)* This is bloody ridiculous...

IRENE. Walk around in them then – go on.

LOUISE *stands and shuffles around in them.*

LOUISE. There! Now do you believe me?

IRENE. Suppose so.

LOUISE *takes the item off.*

IRENE. Now show me the skin on your legs!

LOUISE. Oh for God's sake mum!

LOUISE *obliges, shows* IRENE *her legs, and then hands* IRENE *the trousers.*

IRENE. I'm not wearing those at now that you've worn them.

IRENE *chucks the trousers back at* LOUISE.

LOUISE. Don't be silly. They are perfectly clean.

IRENE. Hmmm. *(she sniffs the clothing)* All right then.

IRENE *struggles dressing herself and* LOUISE *helps her.* LOUISE *surveys her mother's appearance.* IRENE *sits down and picks up teddy again.*

IRENE. What day is it today?

LOUISE. Friday. Shall we brush your...

IRENE. *(interrupting)* Shhhhhhh. The baby's asleep!

LOUISE. *(whispering)* Do you want to wrap baby in a blanket?

IRENE. Yes please.

> LOUISE *picks up a throw from the back of the chair and hands it to* IRENE *who swaddles the teddy very tightly in it.*

IRENE. Night. Sleep tight.

> (IRENE *sits teddy in a little child's chair.*)

LOUISE. Teddy likes that chair.

IRENE. Baby!

LOUISE. Sorry, baby likes that chair. Do you know, I used to love sitting in that.

IRENE. *(looks* LOUISE *up and down)* You're a bit big for it aren't you?

LOUISE. I mean when I was little, at home.

IRENE. Oh. Did you have one like that at home then?

LOUISE. Yes… I did… Shall I do your hair now? Smarten you up a bit?

> IRENE *watches* LOUISE *as she bustles about getting the brush and curlers ready to do* IRENE*'s hair.*

IRENE. How's your Dad?

> *Pause.*

LOUISE. He died… quite a long time ago now.

IRENE. Did he?

LOUISE. Yes.

IRENE. What about your Mum?

> *Long pause.*

LOUISE. She's still alive.

IRENE. Have you seen her lately?

> LOUISE *starts to gently brush her mum's hair.*

LOUISE. Oh, yes. I see her every day.

IRENE. I see my baby every day too.

LOUISE. Good.

IRENE. Does she live local then?

LOUISE. Who?

IRENE. Your mum.

LOUISE. Yes, yes she does… very near.

IRENE. That's nice.

LOUISE. Shall I put some curlers in today? Give your hair a bit of bounce?

IRENE. Yes please.

LOUISE. Okey Dokey then… but remember you need to leave them in till I say so otherwise it doesn't work.

IRENE. All right.

*Pause.*

IRENE. You know, I don't like this hotel anymore. I mean, the foods all right but I don't like it really.

*Pause.*

LOUISE. Don't you?

IRENE. No, sometimes the food makes me ill. I think they do it on purpose.

LOUISE. I think it's quite nice, very tasty. I believe that the chef's got a Michelin star.

IRENE. It used to be good but now it's a bit iffy. You know, that nice young girl that used to be here doesn't live here anymore… she used to come and see me at my bungalow. I really miss her…

*Pause.*

LOUISE. I miss her mum as well.

IRENE. I never knew her.

LOUISE. I did.

IRENE. What was she like?

LOUISE. Oh, you know… a bit bossy at times but she was lovely on the whole.

IRENE. Where did she go? Has she moved away?

LOUISE. Yes… I think she has…she's moved away…

IRENE. To another country? I'd like to do that... live in the sun...

*Pause.*

LOUISE. Yes... she's moved to another country... far, far away.

IRENE. Well I hope she can speak the language. That's very important you know.

LOUISE. She can speak the local language fine, it's just me that has trouble understanding it.

IRENE. When you visit her you mean? You'll have to go to lessons then! Get down to that further education college. They run lots of language classes down there.

LOUISE. I'll do that.

IRENE. What is the local language where your mum lives?

LOUISE. Double Dutch.

IRENE. Really? That's nice.

*Pause.*

IRENE. What day is it today?

LOUISE. Friday *(she has finished putting the curlers in)* There. All done!

IRENE. I need a mirror.

LOUISE *fetches the hand mirror from the coffee table for her.*

IRENE. You've left the curlers in!

LOUISE. I know! Remember, you need to leave them in for a little while, so don't take them out till I say so. Now, I'm going to pop upstairs for a quick shower and I thought you could be getting on with something while I do that. You like to keep busy don't you mum?

LOUISE *hands her mum the can of furniture polish and the duster.*

LOUISE. This room needs a bit of a dust. So it would be really good if you could do that for me. You like dusting don't you mum?

**IRENE** *nods and takes the cleaning materials from* **LOUISE**.

**IRENE**. All right then. I'll do it if you really want me to…

**LOUISE**. Great. I'll be back in a five minutes.

**LOUISE** *exits.*

**IRENE** *starts dusting the room.* **BARBARA CARTLAND** *appears.*

**BARBARA**. What on earth are you doing with that duster darling?

**IRENE**. You know, I really don't like this hotel Barbara. I've never had to help with the cleaning in any other hotel I've been in.

**BARBARA**. I should think not.

**IRENE**. And they don't feed me enough.

**BARBARA**. Why is that?

**IRENE**. They say I haven't paid the bill, but I know I have.

**BARBARA**. Is that why they've got you doing the cleaning darling? Payment in kind?

**IRENE**. I hadn't thought of it like that!

**BARBARA**. Check with your accountant sweetie. He should be able to let you know if you've paid your bill on time or not.

**IRENE**. I will. I'll check.

**BARBARA**. It always pays to keep a tight rein on your finances.

**IRENE**. I do. I do. I'm saving up, but that bloody woman is always looking through my belongings. I'm sure she takes my money when I'm not looking.

**BARBARA**. Good staff are so hard to come by nowadays. You've got to watch them like a hawk.

**IRENE**. I've never had staff before. She's very hard to control.

**BARBARA**. Just let her know who the boss is. Remember, you're in charge.

IRENE. I'm doing my best, but she even tells me what to wear.

BARBARA. The cheeky minx. How appalling!

IRENE. Yes, she tells me what to wear – but she doesn't help me with my make up.

BARBARA. No!

IRENE. No. She knows I can't see to put my eyebrows on all by myself. I like nice eyebrows. I've always looked after them.

BARBARA. So have I darling. A beautiful face is everything to a woman. After forty a woman has to choose between losing her face and her figure. My advice is to keep your face and stay sitting down!

*They both laugh and sit down. We hear the doorbell ring.*

LOUISE. *(Offstage)* I'll get it!

IRENE. *(to* BARBARA*)* She is good at answering the door though. I'll give her that.

*We hear* SHELLEY *offstage talking to* LOUISE.

SHELLEY. Hi Aunty Lou. I've just popped round to see Nan.

LOUISE *and* SHELLEY *enter the room.*

SHELLEY. Mum said you'd both be in this morning. *(to* IRENE*)* Hiya Nan.

IRENE. Who?

SHELLEY. Hiya Nan. How are you today? *(she gives* IRENE *a peck on the cheek)* It's me. Shelley.

IRENE. Shelley?

LOUISE. It's Shelley. Beth's girl... your grandaughter.

IRENE. Oh yes... Shelley... yes... that's a lovely name.

BARBARA. My goodness Irene, she's as pretty as a picture.

IRENE. She's a lot prettier than me.

SHELLEY. Who is?

IRENE. You are! Such a pretty girl.

**SHELLEY**. Am I? It's in the genes! Mum always says that I'm the spit of you Nan.

**LOUISE**. She's right. You're the absolute image of your Nan when she was your age.

**IRENE**. *(to* **BARBARA***)* My age?

**BARBARA**. A woman should never reveal her age darling. One should just pop on diamonds and a beautiful gown, then go forth to dazzle one's public.

**IRENE**. *(to* **BARBARA***)* I'll try that *(to* **SHELLEY***)*. Have you got any diamonds that I could wear?

**SHELLEY**. Diamonds? Not really Nan. But I've brought you some chocolates, your favourite – Black Magic.

> **SHELLEY** *gives* **IRENE** *a box of Black Magic chocolates.*

**IRENE**. Dark chocolate?

**SHELLEY**. Yes.

**IRENE**. *(really pleased)* Black Magic. My favourite. Oh thank you so much... erm...

**SHELLEY**. Shelley...

**IRENE**. Thank you Shelley.

**SHELLEY**. Don't eat them all at once.

**IRENE**. No. I won't... What day is it today?

**SHELLEY**. Friday...

> **IRENE** *busies herself opening the box of chocolates.*
> **LOUISE** *takes the curlers out of her mums hair as the conversation continues.*

**LOUISE**. Aren't you at work today Shelley?

**SHELLEY**. Yes, but I've got some flexi time owing and I just wanted to see Nan before I go in. I haven't been round for ages... I'm sorry Aunty Lou... it's just that nowadays she never remembers who I am and... it upsets me... I'm sorry.

**LOUISE**. Don't apologise. It's lovely to see you.

**IRENE**. Would you like a chocolate?

> **SHELLEY** *goes to take one.*

**SHELLEY**. Oh, yes please...

**IRENE**. *(interrupting)* Not you you greedy little bugger! Don't be so rude. Guests first...

> IRENE *offers* BARBARA *a chocolate. Shelly and* LOUISE *observe her.*

**BARBARA**. No thank you darling. One has to watch one's figure. But do feel free to indulge yourself.

**IRENE**. Are you sure? The Caramel Caress is particularly tasty...

**BARBARA**. Raspberry Heaven is always my personal favourite. That fruity burst of raspberry encased in dark chocolate is soooooo decadent!

**IRENE**. Go on... have one. You know you want to.

**SHELLEY**. Who is she talking to Aunty Lou?

**LOUISE**. I haven't got a clue love, but she seems perfectly happy passing the time of day with whoever it is.

**BARBARA**. No thank you. Have the Raspberry Heaven on me. Go on!

**IRENE**. Alright then *(she selects the chocolate and eats it).* Mmmmm, you're right. That is sooooo decadent!

> SHELLEY *watches as* IRENE *continues to offer* BARBARA *chocolates.*

**SHELLEY**. How do you think she is Aunty Lou?

**LOUISE**. Her memory isn't good at all at the moment.

**SHELLEY**. Is it a lot worse since the last time I saw her?

**LOUISE**. Mmmmm.

**SHELLEY**. Is she still treating teddy like a baby?

**LOUISE**. Yes. Your mum and I are convinced that she must be thinking about the little girl she lost all those years ago. It's tragic really, how it's all come back to haunt her...

**SHELLEY**. *(putting her arm round* LOUISE*'s shoulder)* You're a saint Aunty Lou. You know that don't you?

**LOUISE**. No I'm not. She drives me bloody batty at times.

SHELLEY *checks her watch.*

SHELLEY. Hey, I'll have to dash or I'll be late, but I really want to help if I can. How about if I come over and watch Nan one night a week and you can have a night off? You know, you could go to the pictures or have a girlie night out.

LOUISE. Your mum does a lot for her as well you know. I'm not a prisoner… yet!

SHELLEY. Yeah, but she doesn't have to live with her does she? How about Wednesday nights? I can manage that.

LOUISE. OK. Thanks. Let's give it a try and see how it goes.

SHELLEY. Great! I'll be round next Wednesday at seven o'clock.

LOUISE. Alright, but clear it with your mum first! I'm only letting you do it on the understanding that you can get hold of her if you can't cope.

SHELLEY. It's a deal!

SHELLEY *gives* LOUISE *a peck on the cheek, and then kisses her Nan goodbye.*

SHELLEY. See you on Wednesday Nan.

IRENE. What day is it today love?

LOUISE *looks at* SHELLEY *and gives a big sigh.*

LOUISE AND SHELLEY. *(in unison)* FRIDAY!

SHELLEY. Right, I'm off then.

LOUISE. Shelley, wait… are you in your new car?

SHELLEY. Yes! Come and have a quick nosey… it's on the drive…

LOUISE. Great! I've been dying to see it. Mum, I'll be back in a tic…

LOUISE *and* SHELLEY *exit. The lights change. There is a dreamlike quality to* IRENE *and* BARBARA*'s conversation.*

BARBARA. Is young Shelley still a virgin? You'll have to marry her off quickly before someone deflowers her.

IRENE. Shall I go and ask her?

BARBARA. Better not do that in public sweetie. Just have a discreet word with her as soon as you can.

IRENE. Alright then.

BARBARA. She'll never have a suitor if she's not a virgin... well... not one worth having anyway.

IRENE. Like me you, you mean?

BARBARA. What do you mean darling?

IRENE. I wanted Jim, and I ended up with Bill.

BARBARA. Your husband?

IRENE. Yes.

BARBARA. Weren't you happy with Bill? I thought he was a good husband.

IRENE. Yes, he was, but...

BARBARA. But what?

IRENE. He was so... dull!

BARBARA. How tragic!

IRENE. All he ever talked about was the football and the cricket. We hardly ever went dancing and I loved dancing. I loved to dance.

BARBARA. I do too Irene. Do you know that the two best exercises in the world are making love and dancing, and if I can't manage either then I just walk around the house on tip toes and kick my legs in the air like a can can girl. You should try it. But passion is far and away the best exercise...

IRENE. But there wasn't any...

BARBARA. No passion?

IRENE. No, no passion...

BARBARA. But was he a good provider?

IRENE. Yes.

BARBARA. Did he love his children?

IRENE. He adored them.

BARBARA. Did he stray?

IRENE. Stray?

**BARBARA.** Play away from home?

**IRENE.** *(shocked)* Oh no! He would never have done anything like that, never!

**BARBARA.** Well, you should count your blessings then Irene! Good dull Englishmen make far and away the best husbands. And the reason why Englishmen are the best husbands in the world is because they want to be faithful. A Frenchman or an Italian will wake up in the morning and wonder what girl he will meet. An Englishman wakes up and wonders what the cricket score is!

**IRENE.** That's true. Bill loved his cricket... I wish I'd loved...

**BARBARA.** What?... What?... Did you have a lover Irene? An affair? How exciting!

**IRENE.** No... not a lover.

*A young man nervously enters a spotlight. It is* **JAMES.** *He is dressed in 1960's clothing, aged in his twenties.* **IRENE** *and* **BARBARA** *are in the half light observing. He rings the doorbell.*

**IRENE.** I could see someone through the net curtains. At first I wondered who it was, and then... as soon as he pushed back his hair... I realized it was him.

**BARBARA.** Who? Who could you see?

**IRENE.** It was just like I was looking at Jims face again.

**BARBARA.** Your love child!

**IRENE.** I was afraid to answer the door... but I couldn't stop myself...

*IRENE stands and walks to join* **JAMES** *in the spotlight.*

**JAMES.** Hello.

**IRENE.** Hello.

*Pause.*

**JAMES.** Sorry, sorry... I haven't introduced myself. My name is George Minshull.

IRENE *shakes his outstretched hand, holding it for just a second longer than would be usual.*

IRENE. Hello George.

*Pause as they both look at each other.*

JAMES. I... er... I'm looking for a lady called Irene Jackson?

IRENE. Irene Jackson?

JAMES. Yes. I was told she lived here.

IRENE. Oh?

JAMES. Yes... Irene Jackson. I think her maiden name was Rogers?

IRENE. Rogers?

JAMES. I have got the right address haven't I? This is twenty four Orchard Crescent isn't it?

IRENE. Yes, that's right... number twenty four...

JAMES. And... and... I... have I got the right lady? Are you Irene Jackson?

*Long pause.*

IRENE. Right house...wrong person...

JAMES. Oh... It's just that I was sure that she...

IRENE. She's moved. She used to live here. Before... before we moved here.

JIM. Oh... I see... I'm sorry to have bothered you.

IRENE. It's no bother.

JAMES *turns as if to walk away and then turns back to* IRENE.

JAMES. Could I ask you a really big favour? Could you please pass on my name and address to Mrs Jackson... to Irene... if you have a forwarding address for her? And then she can get in touch with me... if she wants to.

IRENE. I'm not sure if I...

JAMES. Please, please. I would be so grateful if you would do that for me. Here, here. I'll write it down... *(he takes a small notebook and pencil out of his pocket, scribbles his name and address and tears the page out of the notebook to hand to* **IRENE***)...* Can you do that for me, please... please?

**JAMES** *holds the note out to* **IRENE** *who does not take it at first.*

**JAMES**. If... if you could let her know that she might remember me as James. That's really important. Here, I'll just... *(he goes to write his name on the note).*

**IRENE**. No... no... you don't need to do that *(she takes the note)...* I think I can remember that... James.

**JAMES**. It'll all make sense to Irene.

**IRENE**. James... yes... I'm sure it will.

**JAMES** *hold out his hand and shakes* **IRENE**'*s hand.*

**JAMES**. Well, goodbye then, and thank you so much. You don't know how much this means to me.

**JAMES** *exits the spotlight, turning to look at her one last time when she says 'Goodbye', but he does not hear her say his name.*

**IRENE**. Goodbye... *(quietly)* James... *(she looks at the note* **JAMES** *has given her and breaks down in tears. The spot fades and she is back in the dreamlike scene with* **BARBARA***.)*

**IRENE**. My boy... my secret...

**BARBARA**. *(snatching the note off* **IRENE** *to look at)* Ah yes! Secrets! The things we keep hidden from others, hidden from knowledge or view; sometimes concealed, sometimes known only to oneself. Secrets are the kind of mystery that one's readers absolutely adore and...

**IRENE**. *(interrupting loudly)* I won't write it down... I won't... people will find out... Bill might find out.

**BARBARA**. Who cares what boring old Bill thinks!

**IRENE**. I care! And what if my mum finds out... what if mum finds out that I saw him, she'll go mad...

**IRENE** *sits in a chair and starts to sob again. We hear an echo of* **IRENE**'*s voice saying "She'll go mad" as the scene changes back to the current time and* **BARBARA**

*withdraws from the scene. Lights are up again on* **LOUISE**'s *front room.* **LOUISE** *enters.*

**LOUISE.** *(as she enters)* Guess what. Shelley's new car is red – her favourite colour! Mum? Mum... what's the matter?

**IRENE.** I don't want my mum to find out. She said that I mustn't see him. I promised I wouldn't see him again...

**LOUISE.** See who?

**IRENE.** She mustn't find out... I don't want Mum to find out *(sobs quietly)*

**LOUISE.** Find out what? What is it?

**IRENE.** *(scared)* No, I can't tell you... and she mustn't find out... she mustn't...

**LOUISE.** Well she won't will she? She's not with us anymore, remember? She died a long time ago...

**IRENE.** My mum is dead? She's dead?

**LOUISE.** Yes.

**IRENE.** Mums dead? She's dead! When did she die? *(she starts to cry again).*

**LOUISE.** Oh dear! Come here, come on.

(**LOUISE** *tries to comfort her distraught mum but* **IRENE** *pushes her away).*

**IRENE.** Mum's dead. My mum's dead...

**LOUISE.** There there. There's no need to cry... she passed away a long time ago...

**IRENE.** I want my mum back... I want my mum. *(she sobs)* Is your mum still alive?

**LOUISE.** My mum?...

**LOUISE** *stares at her mum as* **IRENE** *picks up teddy in the blanket and exits the scene.* **LOUISE** *watches her go and we hear the echo of* **IRENE**'s *voice saying "Is your mum still alive?"* **LOUISE** *exits as...*

*Lights fade on* **LOUISE**'s *living room. In the darkness we hear the loud screech of brakes and the thud of someone* *being hit by a car. Lights snap up the NHS consulting room.* **BETH** *and the* **CONSULTANT** *are sat talking and the* **CONSULTANT** *is making notes.*

**CONSULTANT**. She was knocked down?

**BETH**. The chap next door was backing out of his drive and she was running out of the bungalow and didn't see that he was reversing out so...

**CONSULTANT**. *(looking at his notes)* So she spent the night in A&E...

**BETH**. Yes. Just one night. She was more bruised than anything else. But then the shock of it all set in a few days later and we had to call out the doctor and the district nurse.

**CONSULTANT**. And she is still living with your sister?

**BETH**. Of course she is! She's not capable of looking after herself, so she's still living with Louise.

**CONSULTANT**. Is Louise with you today?

**BETH**. No... she's is a bit off colour... that's why she hasn't come.

**CONSULTANT**. What about your mothers respite care? How do you both feel that's going?

**BETH**. Well, she's still only going to the care home two days a week... she told them the other day that Louise was keeping her at her house against her will. Talk about deluded!

**CONSULTANT**. Have you considered upping it to three days?

**BETH**. We're hoping to up it to three, but it gets a bit difficult if she is in one of those moods.

**CONSULTANT**. What sort of moods?

**BETH**. You've been to see her there! You know what she's like! Accusing staff of poisoning her or trying to kill her...

**CONSULTANT**. *(looking at his notes)* When did that...

**BETH.** *(interrupting)* And us! Her daughters! The other day she actually passed a note to the postman saying that Louise was trying to kill her!

**CONSULTANT.** That must have been very distressing for Louise.

**BETH.** And the postman. He thinks he's delivering to the Hammer House of Horrors!

*Pause.*

**BETH.** We are really worried Doctor. It's a trial run at the end of the day, and if she carries on deteriorating at this rate then they're not going to be able to cope with her at her current care home for much longer are they?

**CONSULTANT.** Well for the moment…

**BETH.** *(interrupting angrily)* My sister is at the end of her tether! Do you know that? Mum has been giving her hell for weeks. No, I take that back – for months! And the real reason Louise isn't here today is because she can't bear to hear what I'm going to say…

*Long pause.*

**CONSULTANT.** Go on Beth.

**BETH.** It can't go on like this Doctor… we can't go on like this… she's going to have to go into care full time.

**BETH** *breaks down as the lights fade on the scene.* **BETH** *and the consultant exit. Lights come up on* **LOUISE**'s *living room and we hear loud pop music from around 2000/2001 playing.* **SHELLEY** *enters with a Beauty Box, towel, cotton wool and so on. She busies herself setting things out like nail varnishes/ skin care products/ mirror etc on the coffee table and sings along to the music. The mood is upbeat.* **LOUISE** *enters dressed for a night out with the girls.*

**SHELLEY.** Oooh. Look at you in your new gear!

**LOUISE** *does a twirl.* **SHELLEY** *applauds.*

**LOUISE.** Turn it down a bit will you Shelley? Lovely music but a bit loud for me...

**SHELLEY.** *(as she turns the music down)* You know what they say don't you Aunty Lou, if it's too loud.

**LOUISE.** *(interrupting)* You're too old! Yes, yes I know.

**SHELLEY.** Not tonight though. You're looking good girl! I think you might just bag yourself a toyboy.

**LOUISE.** I haven't got the energy for a toyboy. A bit of me time will do just fine thank you.

**SHELLEY.** So who are you meeting up with?

**LOUISE.** Barbara and Marie. We're going to see that new Brad Pitt movie.

**SHELLEY.** He's gorgeous isn't he? I fancy going to see that myself.

**LOUISE.** I won't be too late I hope. I should be home by ten.

**SHELLEY.** You can do your film critic routine for me when you get back.

**LOUISE.** I might chance the girls coming in for coffee afterwards.

**SHELLEY.** Never mind coffee, crack open a bottle of wine.

**LOUISE.** The last time they were here mum came down with all her clothes packed in a suitcase and asked them to take her home with them. She still thinks this hotel isn't up to scratch!

*They both giggle.*

**SHELLEY.** Is Nan out of the bath yet?

**LOUISE.** Yes. All ready for bed. She's just settling teddy down for the night at the moment. She'll probably wander down in a minute... are you sure you're up to this Shelley?

**SHELLEY.** Stop worrying. I'm a big girl now, and mum's on her emergency hotline in case I need any help. Off you go and have fun... go on!

**LOUISE** *gives* **SHELLEY** *a peck on the cheek.*

**LOUISE.** Thanks love. I really appreciate you looking after your Nan for me tonight. See you later.

*LOUISE exits. SHELLEY immediately turns the music up louder and dances around the room. The phone rings. SHELLEY answers the phone.*

**SHELLEY.** Hello?... Hang on a minute...*(she turns the music off)*... Oh hiya mum... She's just left... yeah... yeah... No... no... I'm fine... No! You don't need to come over... Oh for God's sake mum – give it a rest will you! And what do you care anyway – you're the one who wants to put her in a home!

*SHELLEY hangs up abruptly.*

*IRENE enters in her nightie and dressing gown. SHELLEY goes and gives her a hug. BARBARA CARTLAND enters and takes a seat to observe the beauty regime.*

**SHELLEY.** Hi Nan. Come on, come and sit down over here. I've got a great pamper night organised for you.

**IRENE.** *(to BARBARA)* Pamper night?

**BARBARA.** Oh it's just a new fangled expression for one's beauty regime Irene. I think you'll enjoy this.

**SHELLEY.** I'm going to spoil you, you know, do a bit of a facial on you – make your skin nice and soft. And I'm going to paint your nails and toenails! You love having nice nails don't you?

**IRENE.** I do, yes. And nice eyebrows.

*SHELLEY busies herself picking out some nail varnishes from the beauty box.*

**BARBARA.** Now look at me Irene, that's right. Amazing skin my dear for your age, simply amazing. And always remember – if you give the other person your complete attention when they are speaking to you they will invariably remember you as beautiful.

**IRENE.** I'll try that...

*IRENE focuses intently on SHELLEY.*

SHELLEY. Come on, let's pick a colour that you like.

> IRENE *sits down and* SHELLEY *holds up various bottles of nail varnish for her to approve.* IRENE *stares at* SHELLEY *and the nail varnishes intently.*

SHELLEY. This one?

> IRENE *shakes her head and stares at* SHELLEY.

SHELLEY. This one?

> IRENE *shakes her head and continues to stare at* SHELLEY.

SHELLEY. Is there something on my face Nan? *(she picks up the hand mirror)* I had a right zit yesterday – is it still there?

BARBARA. She really should put honey on her spots you know Irene – they will disappear by the morning if she does that...

IRENE. Put honey on them...

SHELLEY. Honey?

IRENE. On your spots. I've got some in the kitchen. *(she goes to get up but* SHELLEY *stops her.)*

SHELLEY. Forget about me Nan – I'm here to make you look beautiful remember! Hey, how about this colour then. Pink – your favourite colour *(she picks up a bottle of bright pink nail varnish).*

BARBARA. And mine darling. What exquisite taste she has Irene, exquisite!

IRENE. *(to* SHELLEY*)* She likes it too *(points at* BARBARA*).*

SHELLEY. *(a little uncertain)* Does she Nan?

> IRENE *smiles and nods.*

SHELLEY. Great! OK – let's start with the face pack first , and while that's working on you I can do your nails, and then we can take the face pack off. What do you think?... Nan, is that OK?

BARBARA. You need to ask her what is in it darling. My advice is to always use the yoke of an egg mixed with almond oil as a face pack. Then allow it to dry and wash off with rose water.

IRENE *smiles and nods.*

IRENE. What's in it?

SHELLEY. What's in what?

IRENE. The face pack. I only allow eggs and almonds on my skin *(nods to* BARBARA*)*.

SHELLEY. Oh... well... right then... *(pretends to read the ingredients)* 'Contains farm fresh eggs and ripe almonds'... is that ok Nan?

BARBARA AND IRENE. *(in unison)* Perfect!

SHELLEY. Great. Sit back in the chair...that's it...

SHELLEY *places a towel round her Nan's neck and applies the grotesquely coloured face pack.*

SHELLEY. I know it feels a bit cold but it does wonders for your skin. Try not to speak while it's on Nan, and I'll wipe it off in about ten minutes. OK? Do you fancy a cup of coffee or a glass of juice or anything while it's drying off?

BARBARA. Certainly not darling. Citrus fruits and coffee are death to the complexion!

IRENE. No thank you. I'll have some tea later on.

SHELLEY. OK. Let's put some nail varnish on your toes now shall we?

SHELLEY *kneels in front of* IRENE *and paints her toenails.* IRENE *is quiet and co-operative.* SHELLEY *hums a tune as she applies the nail varnish to* IRENE*'s toenails.*

BARBARA. Oh – it is so good to see that she is paying attention to your feet Irene! One should always keep ones feet in good order. It makes all the difference to the way you walk, which is very important. The way one walks can often give away one's age.

SHELLEY. Do you remember doing this for me when I was little Nan? I used to love it. Mum wouldn't let me try out her make-up, but when you used to babysit and I'd stay over at yours you'd save all your old lipsticks and nail varnish bottles and I used to have a field day. And the old mascaras.

BARBARA. Mascara? A little beauty tip for you Irene. I always use Meltonian black shoe cream for my eyelashes. It works a treat and is so very very shiny.

SHELLEY. Do you remember our make up sessions Nan? They were great! Our little secret… (SHELLEY *finishes applying nail varnish to one of* IRENE*'s feet.)*

IRENE. I've got a secret.

SHELLEY. Have you Nan?

BARBARA. Don't tell her Irene – remember that you promised your mother not to tell anyone!

IRENE. Sorry… erm…

SHELLEY. Shelley…

　　SHELLEY *waits for* IRENE *to continue. She does not.*

SHELLEY. (SHELLEY *is still applying nail varnish to* IRENE*'s feet)*… and that dressing up box you had was really cool! All those old hats and high heel shoes *(she giggles)* There you go, I've finished your toes. What do you think?

　　IRENE *has a look and shows* BARBARA.

IRENE. Nice… pink. I like pink.

BARBARA. The most beautiful colour in the world my dear.

SHELLEY. I knew you'd love that colour. Shall I do your hands now?

　　IRENE *holds out a hand and relaxes back in her chair and closes her eyes.* SHELLEY *applies the nail varnish.)*

SHELLEY. I can still remember clomping up and down your hall in all your old shoes Nan. I loved the noise they made on the hall tiles… You've got lovely dainty hands Nan, do you know that? Lovely hands… Nan? Nan?

*There is the faint sound of* **IRENE** *and* **BARBARA**
*Cartland snoring.* **SHELLEY** *realises* **IRENE** *is asleep but*
*carries on applying the nail varnish.*

**SHELLEY.** You carry on dreaming while I make you
beautiful...

> **SHELLEY** *finishes applying the nail varnish. She tidies*
> *the make up away, glances across at* **IRENE,** *and then*
> *sits at* **IRENE***'s feet and rests her head on* **IRENE***'s lap*
> *while* **IRENE** *still sleeps. Pause.*

**SHELLEY.** *(big sigh)* She's putting you in a home Nan. Mum
is... I had a right barney with her tonight about it all
just before I came out. How can she do that, how can
she?... You're her mum... her mum...

*Long pause.*

**SHELLEY.** Nan... I've got something to tell you. I'm going
to be a mum soon... I found out last week... you're the
first to know... I know you won't remember, but I just
wanted to tell you tonight... Me and Rob are going
to start looking at some flats for rent next week... I
love Rob to bits...and I know he'll be great with the
baby. *(giggles)* He can't wait!... Mum and Dad... well...
I know they'll be ok about it all once they've got over
the shock... Mum's barks worse than her bite...you
always used to say that to me... I hope it's a boy... I
really fancy a little lad! I can just see him and Rob
playing football together when the baby's older...
Suppose we've gone about it all the wrong way round
but we're both really happy about it...

> **IRENE** *stirs as does* **BARBARA.** **IRENE** *strokes* **SHELLEY***'s*
> *hair.*

**SHELLEY.** Are you awake?

**IRENE.** *(mumbling through her face pack)* Yes... I am... what's
happened to my face?

**SHELLEY.** Oh God, the face pack!. Just hang on while I get
a bowl of water and some cotton wool... stay there...
I won't be a minute. Don't touch it!

*SHELLEY exits.*

*IRENE picks up the mirror and looks at herself. She panics and cries out.*

IRENE. She's poisoned me, she's poisoned my skin. That girl has poisoned me.

*(IRENE stands up.)*

IRENE. Help, help… I've been poisoned, my skin's been poisoned.

BARBARA. Oh do stop panicking Irene. As long as she washes it off with fresh rose water you'll be fine.

*SHELLEY rushes back in with the bowl of water and cotton wool.*

IRENE. No, no… leave me alone you. Leave me alone.

SHELLEY. Nan, it's me… Shelley.

IRENE. I don't care who you are. What have you done to me? Look at my face!

SHELLEY. It's a face pack that's all. Come on, come and sit down and I'll take it off for you.

IRENE. You've done this on purpose!

SHELLEY. I've done it to make your skin nice and soft that's all. You used to like having facials. Remember?

IRENE. Did I?

SHELLEY. Yes…

*Pause as IRENE calms down. SHELLEY guides her back to her chair and sits her down.*

SHELLEY. There you go. You settle down there and I'll take it off.

IRENE. What's in that bowl? Is it fresh rose water?

SHELLEY. Fresh rose water? Er… yes… yes… fresh rose water…

BARBARA. Wonderful! Just sit down and relax Irene.

*IRENE sits down. SHELLEY takes the face pack off and chats as she does so.*

**SHELLEY**. Is that all right for you? Not too hot?

**IRENE**. Mmmmmm.

**SHELLEY**. Good. Just relax and sit back… it doesn't take long…you'll look about twenty one when I've finished with you.

*IRENE giggles. SHELLEY finishes taking off the face pack.*

**SHELLEY**. There you go Nan. All done! You look great. I'll just get rid of this bowl.

*SHELLEY exits with the bowl. IRENE looks at herself in the mirror and shows BARBARA.*

**BARBARA**. You look wonderful darling. Now remember to wash your face in cold water every morning – and smile! Breathe deep, dance, walk and run. Laugh, enjoy yourself, have fun! You are lovely when you smile, just lovely…

*BARBARA withdraws from the scene as SHELLEY re-enters.*

*SHELLEY re-enters and picks up the TV remote control and switches on the TV.*

**SHELLEY**. Shall we see what's on the goggle box? I think it's one of those talent shows you like.

**IRENE**. No *(she grabs the remote control from SHELLEY)* No, I don't want the TV on.

*She presses the button on the TV remote but presses the wrong button and the sound becomes uncomfortably loud.*

**SHELLEY**. No Nan. Give it here, come on, I'll turn it off for you.

*IRENE carries on pressing buttons and the channels switch from one to another at an alarming rate with the sound at full blast.*

**IRENE**. They're in there watching me – I know they are! They're always watching me…

*She throws the remote on the floor in frustration.*

IRENE. *(shouts)* They're watching me. SWITCH IT OFF!

> **SHELLEY** *grabs the remote and turns the TV off abruptly.*

> *Long pause.*

IRENE. I'm going to see if my baby is alright…

> **IRENE** *exits. Pause.* **SHELLEY** *picks up the telephone and rings a number.*

SHELLEY. Hi. It's Shelley… yeah… no, no, you don't need to come over… I'm ok… well, just about… I wanted to say… I'm really sorry about that barney tonight… it was my fault… I'm sorry mum… I love you too…

> *Light fades on the* **LOUISE**'s *living room as* **SHELLEY** *tidies away the make-up box and exits in silence. In the momentary blackout we hear the sound of a phone ringing out. Then a spotlight comes up on* **BETH** *holding the telephone as she rings a succession of care homes and becomes more and more despondent. After each sentence the spotlight blacks out momentarily and in the blackout we hear the phone ringing out as she rings another care home.*

BETH. So you don't feel that your establishment is suitable for her then?

> *Blackout.*

What if we came out and had a look round?… No?… Oh…

> *Blackout.*

So it would be fine for her current condition but not if she deteriorates further? I see, so she'd have to move to another establishment at that stage?… no… no… not ideal for her really.

> *Blackout.*

Perfect!… No vacancies at the moment?… How long is your waiting list?

> *Blackout.*

Well, she's not violent at the moment... well... I say not violent...

*Blackout.*

It sounds ideal for her but... the problem is... you're such a long way away... yes, we would like to see her regularly... we would.

*Blackout.*

What sort of activities do you do for people in her condition?... Is that all?... I see...

*Blackout.*

Yes, yes... great! We'll be round on Thursday for a look round 10am. Wonderful. See you then...

*Blackout.*

Louise? I think I've cracked it! 'Green Meadows'... yes... it's only five miles away! We can go round on Thursday morning... I know... I know... now don't get upset... take a deep breath and sit down with a cup of coffee... It's going to be fine... we can talk it all through tonight when mums asleep... come on now... be strong. See you later.

**BETH** *hangs up the phone and cries.* Bewitched, Bothered and Bewildered *plays as the spot fades on her. Lights come up on* **LOUISE**'s *living room.* **LOUISE** *and* **BETH** *enter carrying a couple of boxes full of* **IRENE**'s *old photographs and paperwork/letters.*

LOUISE. I suppose this is the last leg then – sorting all of these odds and ends out.

BETH. Should be a doddle after all the other paperwork we've had to deal with.

LOUISE. Let's make two piles then –'bin' and 'keep' ?

BETH. Sounds good to me *(she indicates two spaces on the coffee table)* 'bin' over here, and 'keep' over there.

LOUISE. Okey dokey... we can take all the old photos in for mum when we go to see her at Green Meadows tomorrow.

**BETH**. Good idea – she'll like that.

*They start to sort through the paperwork. Momentary silence.*

**LOUISE**. How's Shelley getting on?

**BETH**. She's going for her check-up next week.

**LOUISE**. Is Rob going with her?

**BETH**. Course he is, talk about the proud Dad!

**LOUISE**. Hey, look at this... me and you at junior school *(she shows* **BETH** *an old photograph).*

**BETH**. Look at the state of that haircut! What a sight. I look like I've had a bowl put on my head.

**LOUISE**. And this one... Dad... before he had his stroke. He was always so smart...

*Pause as they both look at the photograph.*

**LOUISE**. How's the proud Grandad to be?

**BETH**. Geoff? Still as pleased as punch. He thinks the world of Rob so he's happy Shelley's settling down with him. Mind you, that house they're renting needs all sorts doing to it. So Geoff's been down there with his power tools morning noon and night – they must be sick of the sight of him!

*LOUISE shows* **BETH** *another photograph.*

**LOUISE**. Look – Mum when she was a teenager! I love the dresses she used to wear. Your Shelley is the image of her.

**BETH**. I know.

**LOUISE**. Who's that lad with her... Do you know?

**BETH**. No, but he's a handsome so and so isn't he?

**LOUISE**. Looks like she had a taste of romance before she met Dad then.

*They both giggle.*

**LOUISE**. Have you decided what title you're going for yet – Nan, Gran, Granny or Grandma?

**BETH.** I think I'll make that decision when she's had the baby.

**LOUISE.** I'm sticking with Aunty Lou – Great Aunty Lou's a bit of a mouthful for a little lad. Have they picked a name for him yet?

**BETH.** No, not yet.

**LOUISE.** I was surprised they decided to find out the sex of the baby.

**BETH.** Well you know what our Shelley's like – no patience – and she wants to sort out the nursery. It'll be a riot of blue by the time she's finished with it...

> **LOUISE** *looks at a letter in the pile of old photos and paperwork.*

**LOUISE.** God, how much old stuff has mum hung on to ! This looks like a personal letter... from... 1965...

**BETH.** 1965?

**LOUISE.** I wonder why she's kept this all these years? There's one for the bin pile...

> *She goes to put it on the bin pile.*

**BETH.** Read it and find out.

**LOUISE.** Pardon.

**BETH.** Read the letter and find out.

**LOUISE.** Beth!

**BETH.** What?

**LOUISE.** You can't do that. It's private.

**BETH.** Oh...give it here you soft thing...

> *She takes the letter from* **LOUISE** *and opens it. As* **BETH** *and* **LOUISE** *look at the letter the lighting changes to a spot on the two sisters, and four other spots on the stage into which the following characters slowly enter in the following order as* Bewitched, Bothered and Bewildered *softly plays:* **IRENE** *with her pink hat and coat on over her clothes and carrying teddy wrapped in a blanket,* **JAMES** *in 1965 clothing ,* **YOUNG IRENE** *in 1940's clothing carrying baby* **JAMES** *wrapped in a*

*shawl, and* **BARBARA** *Cartland.* **JAMES** *should be stood in a spot on a raised dais so that he can be seen looking at* **IRENE** *with her teddy as he speaks and the music fades out…*

**JAMES.** Dear Irene, I want to write 'Dear Mum' because I know in my heart that it was you I spoke to when I stood on your doorstep last month. Something about how you said my real name… James… has stayed with me since that day, and I can't forget it. I just wanted to let you know that my life with my adoptive parents has turned out well and that I am loved and cared for. I know from them that you were younger than I am now when you had me, and how hard it must have been for you to give me up. I think about you every day since we met, and want you to know that I want nothing but the best for you, and hope that you have as happy a family life as I have. You mustn't worry that I will come searching for you again, but if you ever feel that you want to contact me I would love to hear from you. Look after yourself Mum, your loving son, James.

*All the spots except the one on* **BARBARA CARTLAND** *fade to a half light as* **BARBARA** *has the last word:*

**BARBARA.** As all my readers know, the heroine is always at the centre of my work, and my usual recipe is that there should always a happy ending, but one can also leave people wondering if things will ever be resolved…

*Spots fade to blackout as* Bewitched, Bothered and Bewildered *fades up.*

### The End

**Property Plot –**

Act 1

NHS consulting room (p1)
Living room reading a book (p1)
Doctor's notes (p1)
Hanky (p2)
Romantic novel (p7)
Shopping bag (p8)
Tray with two china cups of tea with saucers and a
    mug of tea (p9)
Meal on a tray (p11)
Bowl of scrambled eggs (p11)
Spoon (p11)
Plate of toast (p11)
Torch (p13)
Watch (p15)
Hairbrush (p15)
Irene's handbag (P15)
Pink notebook (p17)
Pen (p18)
Baby swaddled in a shawl (p23)
Nightdress (p25)
Blanket (p25)
Chair (p25)
Torch x2 (p26)
Mobile Phone (p28)
Lamplight (p32)

Costumes:
Barbara Cartland: glittering vision in pink (p1)
Irene: smart conservative clothes (p7)
Barbara Cartland: full pink regelia (p7)
Beth: Anorak (p8)
Irene: Nightclothes and dressing gown (p13)
Louise: Coat over her clothes (p13)
Irene: Coat over her nightdress, wearing wellies (p26)
Beth: Coat over her pyjamas, wearing wellies (p26)

Irene: Barefoot with a nightdress (p29)

## Act 2

Mug of tea (p33)
Hand mirror (p33)
Coffee table (p33)
Box of curlers and a comb (p33)
Duster (p33)
Can of furniture polish on coffee table (p33)
Teddy bear (p33)
Trousers (p34)
Throw (p35)
Little child's chair (p35)
Box of black magic chocolates (p40)
Small notebook (p44)
Pencil (p44)
Beauty Box (p48)
Towel (p48)
Cotton wool (p48)
Nail varnish (p48)
Skin care products (p48)
Mirror (p48)
Face pack (p51)
Bowl of water (p53)
TV (p54)
TV remote control (p54)
Telephone (p55)
Couple of boxes full of Irene's old photographs and
    paperwork/letters (p56)
Baby wrapped in a shawl(p58)
Raised dais(p58)

Costumes:
Barbara Cartland: A shimmering vision in pink (p33)
Irene: Hat, coat, underwear, a blouse, cardigan and
    socks, but no trousers (p33)
Louise: Nightclothes and dressing gown (p33)
James: 1960s clothing (p43)
Louise: dressed for a night out with the girls (p48)

Irene: Nightie and dressing gown (p49)
Irene: Pink hat and coat over her clothes (p58)
James: 1965 clothing (p58)
Young Irene: 1940s clothing (p58)

## Sound Effects

### Act 1

Bewitched, Bothered and Bewildered by Ella
    Fitzgerald (p1)
Music swells again (p1)
Disembodied, gentle voice of her interrogator Dr
    Johnson (p4)
Faint echo of the consultant saying "when you say
    deteriorate what do you mean?" (p7)
Off stage - Beth entering the bungalow (p7)
Faint echo of Irene shouting 'I don't want the
    fucking eggs" (p12)
Doorbell ringing loudly (p13)
This sound fades (p13)
The doorbell is still ringing (p13)
Doorbell stops (p14)
Woman singing Abide With Me by Henry Francis Lyte
    on the radio (p14)
Singing stops abruptly (p14)
Faint echo of Irene saying "Promise me you won't
    take my money" (p16)
Echo of the consultant's voice reading this line (p18)
Echo of consultant's voice fades away (p18)
Interrupted by sudden sound of a woman singing
    Abide With Me on the radio (p19)
Music stops abruptly (p20)
Very faint sound of 1940s dance music swells and
    then recedes (p21)
Dance music swells again (p21)
Music ends (p21)
1940s version of Bewitched, Bothered and Bewildered
    plays and fades (p21)

Sound of the band music swells as the moment
   unfreezes (p22)
Music swells again (p23)
Irene's words 'he was adopted of course' echo across
   the stage (p24)
The echo fades out as Irene speaks (p24)
Bewitched, Bothered and Bewildered is heard (p25)
Music continues to play (p25)
The music becomes discordant and is drowned out
   by a woman loudly singing Abide with Me (p25)
The singing suddenly stops (p25)
Abide with Me starts up again (p25)
Abide with Me stops abruptly (p25)
Tapping on the windows is heard very softly but
   insistently. (p25)
Slowly grows louder and louder until it is unbearable
   for Irene (p25)
The loud tapping becomes intermingled with the
   sound of a baby crying (p25)
The crying becomes louder (p25)
The crying grows unbearably loud (p26)
Sudden Silence (p26)
Mobile phone rings (p28)
Police Siren (p30)
Car door open and shut (p30)
As lights fade Bewitched, Bothered and Bewildered
   plays (p32)


## Act 2


Bewitched, Bothered and Bewildered Plays (p33)
Spot and romantic music fades (p33)
Doorbell rings (p39)
He rings the doorbell (p43)
Hear an echo of Irene's voice saying "She'll go mad"
   (p45)
Hear the echo of Irene's voice saying 'is your mum
   still alive?' (p46)

We hear the loud screech of breaks and the thud of
    someone being hit by a car (p46)
Loud pop music from around 2000/2001 playing
    (p48)
Turns the music up louder (p49)
The phone rings (p49)
Faint sound of Irene and Barbara Cartland snoring
    (p52)
TV sound becomes uncomfortably loud (p54)
TV sound on full blast (p54)
Hear the phone ringing out (p55)
Phone ringing out (p55)
Bewitched, Bothered and Bewildered plays (p56)
Bewitched, Bothered and Bewildered softly plays
    (p58)
Music fades out (p58)
Bewitched, Bothered and Bewildered fades up (p58)

## Lighting

### Act 1

Spotlight (p1)
Momentary blackout (p1)
Lights come up (p1)
Dim light (p1)
Sudden sharp spotlight (p4)
Sudden blackout (p5)
Lights fade (p7)
Lights fade up (p7)
Lights fade (p12)
and come up (p12)
Lights fade (p13)
and come up (p13)
Lights are not on (p13)
Switches on light (p13)
Lights start to fade (p16)

Louise in spotlight (p15)
Lights fade up (p15)
Lights fade on the room (P18)
Consultant is now stood in spotlight (p18)
Spotlight fades (p18)
Lights fade up (p18)
Lights dim (p21)
Spotlight (p21)
Spotlight (p22)
Lights fade (p23)
Spotlight fades up (p23)
Spot on her fades (p24)
Lights gently fade up to a half light and a soft mist
    swirls around the stage (p25)
Blackout (p26)
Lights come up (p26)
Flashing Lights (p30)
Headlights of a car (p30)
Lamplight which fades slowly (p32)
Lights fade (p32)


Act 2

Spotlight fades up (p33)
Lights come up (p33)
Lights change (p42)
Spotlight (p43)
Irene and Barbara are in the half light (p43)
James in the spotlight (p43)
James exits the spotlight (p45)
Spot fades (p45)
Lights are up again (p45)
Lights fade (p46)
Lights snap up (p46)
Lights fade on the scene (p48)
Lights come up (p48)
Light fades (p55)

Momentary blackout (p55)
Spotlight comes up on Beth (p55)
Spotlight blacks out (p55)
Blackout (p55)
Blackout (p55)
Blackout (p55)
Blackout (p55)
Blackout (p55)
Blackout (p55)
Blackout (p56)
Blackout (p56)
Spot fades on her (p56)
Lights come up (p56)
Lighting changes to a spot on the two sisters (p58)
Four other spotlights on the stage - into which the
    characters walk on (p58)
All the spots except that of Barbara Cartland fade to
    a half light (p58)
Spot fades to blackout (p58)

Lightning Source UK Ltd.
Milton Keynes UK
UKOW06f0752040615

252882UK00001B/7/P